Searching For Good

Searching For Good

A POETRY TRIPTYCH

Lee Mark Sawatzky

To order additional copies of this book, contact:
Xlibris Corporation
1-888-795-4274
www.Xlibris.com
Orders@Xlibris.com
100247

Contents

THERE WILL BE A TOMORROW
songs and poems to 2006

OTHERNATURAL
poems to 2008

Forward

It's been rather a while since I had my immersion course in the poetry of Lee Sawatzky. In a word—thanks! It's not that often I get into the poetic headspace in my reading, but when I do, it's the best. Thanks for the push into that unique way of refining the world that is called poetry.

Having been a witness to some of your earlier scribblings (I still remember your "sweatered Moses") it was something to realize you have found a voice that is most certainly your own. It sneaks up on you. It is not deceptively matter of fact. It is matter of fact. It has a cumulative effect, all that no-nonsense. The world clarified. An account given. The poetic form assumed to give economy to an observation, a story, a conjecture. It is not an encryption of the intangible, not a decoding of the ineffable. Where it is abstruse it is about the building blocks of meaning. Where it is a story it is about what happened—not just the outward event but also what happened, or may have happened within the observer and the observed. The story does not stand in the place of some greater meaning. If a greater meaning is there, it is not left for us to infer, but addressed directly. It is honest, this poetry. This should not be unique, but it strikes me as such, because the voice is its own. One closes the book ready to observe one's own story with greater clarity.

A confession. I quite consciously wrote the above without having "refreshed my memory" of your poems—four or five months have passed since my immersion in them last summer. What you see above is the residue they left me. I checked in again with a few of the poems from *Othernatural*. . . . I wanted to see if my memory, my spontaneous review, matched the reality.

It does, in the broad strokes, but I would cavil at a few things—first, actually, they are "deceptively" matter of fact. You have a way of throwing things wide open at the end of a poem which have been up to that point a series of observations that follow from a clearly stated premise. I guess that's why they are poems, not theses. Another thing is that those "building blocks of meaning" I see within them are not placed as a mason would place them. They are juxtaposed in surprising ways. Open spaces are left between them. I guess those would be called windows, a place for the reader to catch sight of his own perceptions. Also, what I said about the poetic form giving "economy" does not capture another aspect of some of the poems.

Sometimes the poetic form allows you to elaborate on the premises and implications, the ironies and the underbelly, etc., of what might be at its heart a fairly commonplace observation. Like a realist painting which asks you to see, in detail, what you look at every day.

In looking at them again, I was also reminded of why it took some time to work through them. Because many of them will jump-start an inner-dialogue with my own opinions/observations that I will want to pursue, some refinement of my own understanding being the fruit of the poem for me, if only I take the time to reach for it. So down goes the book until next time . . . .

R. Goertz

going north

POEMS TO 2011

going north

beautiful yet unforgiving,
long term approaches, and
lingering effects:
the mysteries, cold this time of year, in God's country

empty white fields and broken black fence lines,
frozen exhaust clouds,
crunching, resistant snow,
a low level panic to get back indoors

up here in the almighty north
justice is the exact price you
would expect yourself to pay
as you think on the help you will need some day

. . . you go to family gatherings
to seek forgiveness
which can be instantly available
or can accumulate slowly

you also go to family gatherings
to bless, if that's the right word,
and, yes,
to try to forgive

as your people circle
the best moments are formed by laughter
from the revisited comic tropes
made new by time

I've been in the unreal city so long
I have forgotten
the natural workings
used in the great metaphors

condemning the all-access portals
of t.v. and the internet,
what's left when you take away
taste, temperature and consequences?

sparkling world

who doesn't want
a sparkling world,
you know,
a world that's like the world we imagine

the problem is
we constantly encounter
bad situations, many we've created ourselves,
and whacked people

not to minimize
the glorious times we have
shaking down boogie street
and bouncing off the sights of funky town

but a large part
of each day happens to be spent
racing out of alleys and breathlessly asking
for directions out of here

I am undoubtedly miles
from the agreed-to understanding
of Luke 22:35-36, which is in time
just prior to the crucifixion:

"Then Jesus asked them,
'When I sent you
without a purse, bag or sandals,
did you lack anything?'

'Nothing,' they answered.
He said to them, 'But now
if you have a purse,
take it,

and also a bag; and
if you don't have a sword,
sell your cloak
and buy one.'"

I had been away
from this passage for long enough
that it struck me anew
when I read it again recently

some months later,
I had a chance encounter
with a retired soldier
who quoted these verses to me

I do not understand Christ's words
as solely confirming
the prophesy that He
would be among the lawless

instead, I read them as
a statement about
how our difficult, even dangerous, world
demands self-preservation

. . . I align this passage
with Christ's earlier
recognition of the inevitability of
the wheat and the tares (weeds) . . .

perhaps a half-dozen times
in my life
I have had an overwhelming fear
that comes from the presence of great evil

at these most black times,
which have always occurred
at day's end
and when I am alone . . .

. . . I feel I am positioned
immediately next to an approaching, living darkness
and there is nothing
I can do to defend myself

these are not panic attacks
to be calmed by therapy
they are, instead, related to the sense
that someone is looking at you

so I turn to God,
not in a litany
but in brief, simple prayer, and
make a heart-true request for His protection

which He has always provided

other poetry

as far as I can figure out
poetry
is supposed to
make us think

with ideas, word choice,
description ("fair phrase"),
and unexpected
connections

and, of course,
the descriptions
in a poem should never
overwhelm its theme

on this standard
poetry can be found
everywhere,
least often in a formal collection

listen to the poetry
of the sports announcer
searching (and often finding)
one more way, a better word . . .

. . . to describe a home run,
a long range shot on goal,
dribbling/dangling,
an on-field collision

there are even snippets
in wine reviews
despite the incongruity
between taste and description

of course,
any good story-teller
now and again, sometimes knowingly,
slips into the beautiful form

there is less to recommend
in the poetry found in advertising
as mercenary phrases
are written only to be remembered

contrast the value
of the honest, fumbled words of an older person
who must say things differently
because of a disappearing vocabulary

even more dear to my heart
is the poetry
regularly recited by common folk
in small group prayers

their respectful entreaties
often include, what seem
to be to me at least,
precise theological expression

listening, I am reminded
of the soul-deep assuredness
that life has a greater meaning: it is more than
love, friends, family, nature and art

it makes sense that the best setting
for poetry would be
in a conversation
with the very world-maker

what you say to God
cannot be improved
with editing or with
ever more information

whether a prayer of thanks
for the Spring-green joy of life
or a request for the early death
of a slow dying elder . . .

. . . the best words are pure words,
not chosen for artifice or guile
but said in response to the greatest belief,
belief in the Divine

what is there to recommend

the torsion bar
between what I admire
and what I am dead set against
may not hold firm

there it was, in vivid colours
a cross-page advertisement
claiming my attention
for the next book I had to read

if I liked this author
and that author,
the author being promoted
was the very author for me

it turns out I have read this author
and that author
and they are no slouches
for plot and provocation

in fact they are
decidedly top-notch crime writers,
to be read on long flights, whose storylines
are thrilling, layered and always engaging

the problem is
both the benchmark books,
and obviously the touted book,
are steeped in crime

criminals/bad people
(allowing that, by degree,
they are us and we them)
are the people I try hardest to avoid

                              I read somewhere that
                            Agatha Christie became
             disillusioned with writing about crime
               after the horrors of World War II

is reading about crime, fine?
I guess so, as long as
I do not have to actually interact
with any of the imagined criminals

as I looked over the ad
I could tell by the picture of the book's cover
that the storyline could be expected
to have its share of sex

sex, together with the thrill of jeopardy,
is the sugar content (the MSG, the carbs)
in most books about crime;
sugar can make almost anything tasty!

we are all sugar fiends
we never have enough sugar,
at least when we are young;
but, in time, we learn of its affects

. . . a world of liberties:
where everything shocking
is allowed, discussed,
published, and promoted . . .

I don't want
to live out my life
anywhere near the new novel's world
because I've seen what crime does

I'm not confident that you can fully shelter
the living, breathing moral compass of criminal lawyers
who commit to saving
the individual from the state

I fear for police officers
hired to push back at crime's force,
who have to re-set the value of life
as each day darkens into night

how about the communities
that are shell-shocked by incidents of nearby crime,
their good citizens worn down
by constantly being on watch

and what about the degraded morality
of the families of thieves, and that
of the teachers teaching the children of those families,
and the neighbours of those families . . .

despite it all,
the sugar, the adrenalin,
in this, the latest great crime novel
beckoned to all of us on the metro

it made we wonder
what there is to recommend
about a book of poems
that has no sugar at all

'round again

'round again
'round again
I guess I should go 'round again

I guess I should go 'round again
to the places where I source
the word-folk art that has become the best way
for me to learn

I know a lot more than I used to
like how the first thought never changes
and that my pleasurable task is to refine
the presentation, as many thoughts complete slowly

editing again and again
each time feeling certain of the result, but accepting
that it always takes a day or two to find out if the change
is absolutely right or absolutely wrong

I can't stress this enough:
if the idea is classic (to me), worthy
then in a few days the changes will lessen
and in a few more days will stop, forever

I also can't over emphasize
how each little study takes me away
from everyone and every event,
and, really, everything productive in the here and now

to separate out
to blind myself to the ongoing
for the purpose of trying to record
something that seems important

inertia, which I guess you would now call post-modern inertia
needs to be startled to consider changing its state
and even then it takes the exact right opening line
to convert a push into a start

"I guess I should go 'round again"
this line that seemed to have potential was un-beckoned
the words simply showed up
like a daydream with no surrounding dream

in their own way the words refer to a duty,
the duty to keep on beginning
they also acknowledge a routine, in that parts of the route,
if taken, will feel familiar

I also sense hope in the background,
hope of at least the partly new
(else why would you go 'round again?)
recharged, the journey continues

'round again

hunger and thirst

"'Blessed are those who hunger and thirst
for righteousness . . ." Matthew 5:6

the common discomforts
of hunger for food and thirst for water
are easily
recognized

yet not all hunger
is for food
and not all thirst
is for water

a suspended penny
recently dropped
(yet one more incomplete thought
resolved in night's active subconscious)

I began to understand when it was I—
in what environment I—
hunger and thirst
for righteousness

it turns out I need to be
uncomfortable, i.e. not in a state of satisfaction,
to hunger and thirst
for the pursuit of righteousness

this contrasts with the bucolic setting
that I expect I assumed was key
to contemplating
higher standards of conduct

I seek God and his standards most
when I am too troubled
to enjoy almost anything,
yes, almost anything

typically this occurs
as a result of concerns about
what might follow from something I've done
or been caught up in

even though my times of trouble
often last but a handful of bad hours
luckily, they usually last long enough
for my discomfort to catalyze . . .

. . . into the special hunger
and thirst that can
only be satisfied by
acknowledging this is God's world

           I hesitate to comment,
           but so many times I have seen interest wane
           when anything about the othernatural
           is introduced in a conversation

           is it stark disbelief—humans the
           latest, soulless dinosaur iteration?
           mind-numbingly beyond our understanding?
           or, do we just want to stay in charge?

until I remember that God creates life
—or until I become distracted again—
I remain unhappy;
hungry and thirsty

when I recognize
my hunger and thirst for what they are
I begin to regain peace
by humbling myself and praying

I may only hunger and thirst
for righteousness in times of
sadness, fear and pain
. . . even so, I am blessed

the bike ride

I sometimes think about
the innumerable, anonymous explorers
who sailed east to west (and west to east)
before Columbus

for how many
other failed adventurers,
be it because of a gale,
or ship or storage malfunction, . . .

. . . should we properly add
a mute stanza to
the great,
unwritten, collective elegy

you choose: foolhardy or courageous.
maybe what we did as men
is what we will always do:
set out daily on untested routes

. . . .

my profession is like
walking a tightrope between
two high buildings
in the wind and rain

one complication
is that you can never be certain
whether or not
the insurance safety net is in place

there is uncertainty about this
because your work
often lives on, untested,
for years and years

so you may not find out
until many years later
that you fell
a long time ago

. . .

"But if it was going
to be that easy wouldn't you just
put money in
a gumball machine?"

. . .

or . . . my vocation is
a bicycle ride like no other;
a bike ride
from hell really

you see, this bike ride
is not from town to town
no, it is a bike ride
that cannot end

to stop for a moment would be
to leave unfinished
the overlooked and ripening files
of clients who, yes, trusted you

equally important, to stop would be
to extinguish your income
while innumerable expenses
continued unabated

so each day
you get back on the horse . . .
go back to the office
that scared you so badly

. . .

and then you have
a health crisis
and suddenly everything else seems
manageable, easy really

. . .

or . . . my job is like
hanging around a busy crossing
waiting for the inevitable
train wreck

no one wants to be around
a train wreck, especially any of us;
when a train wreck occurs
people look for someone, anyone to blame

. . .

I recently had a detailed dream
wherein I was waiting to be sentenced
for a trumped up charge
in a generic, authoritarian state

the dream broke and I awoke
and lay in the dark
with a sense of freedom
as powerful as if I had been freed from jail

. . .

or . . . what I do
is equivalent to trying to empty
a magical vending machine
that is always full

each time you pull out a can
another can, another file,
another concern,
takes its place

and, of course,
you can only flat-out worry
about something
for so long

. . .

so many decisions
are beyond deciding
yet scant leeway can be given
to the high-riders on this legal-bus

. . .

there is but a small difference
between trying to plot my career
and trying to reconcile
the absurdities of life

whether at work or play
we walk tight ropes,
ride forsaken bikes, wait for trains to collide,
hope that our very last concern will disappear

when I find myself thinking too long about
whether my resolution will be
on hard ground, near twisted metal,
or exposed to fire or ice . . .

. . . I grab at my bootstraps
and remind myself, in faith,
that I am here
otherwise than through chance

and I remember the promise that nothing
can keep God's love from me,
to paraphrase the favorite Bible passage
for those my age

the shrinking man (on grace)

I am as tall as I ever was
but I know
from those ageing around me
that I will soon lose height

several of the men I knew years ago
were established by their size
I've seen them lately
and they all seem smaller

I remember being cautioned
about tackling
one of them in a football game;
I expect it would now be a fair contest

since I am not yet the shrinking man
I have decided
to keep moving forward while I can,
and to try to take on the more difficult issues

my prevailing thought is that, if nothing else,
at least I'll do a better job today
than I could
tomorrow

in fact, unless I am unable
to be honest with myself
(or have forgotten)
I see things ever more clearly

how about . . . grace,
which is particularly difficult,
and yet relevant given the innumerable
differences between us

to begin, I have become
more distrustful of people
as I age, which
is probably universal

(I had never previously
considered moving to a monastery
but lately I've had this thought
in the face of minor day-to-day conflict . . .

. . . though with some sadness I confess
that I now see a monastery almost as much
as a place to get away from man
as it is a place to find God)

grace:
what to expect from others, if anything
how much to accept in others, if everything:
the grace wars

on the one hand
there is the world I am quick to assess,
both as to how it is I see it
and how it is I would improve it

on the other,
there is simply the way things are
absolutely everything continuing apace
without my unneeded judgment

I discussed grace with a friend a while ago;
this friend
often has something to say
beyond saying nothing . . .

. . . young people,
and even some adults,
have been known to, years later,
thank him for speaking up

we reviewed
that grace is not really about doing
whatever it is you want to do
it is, instead, undeserved love

we are directed to extend this grace to others in turn
but at no point in the Great book
is grace ever described
as being total freedom

among other reasons, this is because
uncontrolled actions will inevitably
cause harm to us, our spouses,
our children, and our community

my friend's thoughts
helped me come to learn in part
a lesson that undoubtedly applies to more than
the difficult issue of grace

when at all possible,
I should try not to focus on either
the pure theology or the practical implications
of the matter at hand . . .

. . . rather, I need to trust that
most questions will resolve on their own,
if, and only if, I focus solely on
my pursuit of God, through Christ

while this may appear to be
an out and out side-stepping
I find support for this approach
in Proverbs 3:5:

"Trust in the Lord with all your heart
and lean not on your own understanding;
in all your ways acknowledge him
and he will make your paths straight."

back to grace:
as I think on it today
I am increasingly convinced that
none of us can attain substantive grace on our own

each of us needs
God's divine guidance to, for example,
better appreciate memorable
yet self-interested individuals;

or, to begin to accept those with
one, but not both of the essential qualities of
a becoming personality
and life knowledge;

or, now thinking about
the shrinking man,
to disrupt recurring thoughts
of mistake and disappointment

ebbing connections

driving on a cold, wet road
where to, it doesn't matter, because in this direction
for the entire circumference of the world,
there's no place I really care to go

I know, though, that I need
to put my arm around your thin shoulders
and let simple touch
explode what I've been imagining

blessed me,
I have been told the great truth
and yet rebellion continues
to rise up out of dark layers of thought

to myself I say, again:
you can architect, engineer and construct
but regardless of whether or not the math allows it
things are either right or they are not

most of what we do is either fair or unfair
it is self-evident, naturally (un)just,
a forest green standard of what's right . . .
according to my conscience . . . in my heart of hearts

in pure contradiction, it is my own heart
that keeps dragging me back,
back to my capacities and pleasures,
the usual gang of inclinations

but when these, my so-called friends, gather
I become restless, and, after tossing and turning,
I eventually remind myself to check the plumb line:
honor God and man

but long before that I often seek to distract myself;
my friend says that when he plays poker
he can disappear for hours,
which, apparently, is his ambition

more powerful yet:
"bind yourself in love, and anon!"
. . . love can be as powerful as moving
from the suburbs to a penthouse in the city

up here on the 30th floor,
when Faust looked out on the other elevated lights
in the middle of the night
he felt like he was sleeping in the clouds

in the first few weeks
he eagerly strode to the window every morning
to take in yet another new and amazing sight
. . . but in time he didn't bother

longing

"The eye never has enough
of seeing, nor the ear its fill
of hearing . . . He has set
eternity in the hearts of
man." Ecclesiastes 1:8 and
3:11

I have read that on average
poets lose the edge to their ability
by the time they reach
the age of fifty

that's a pity
because though still light years away
I feel I am closer than ever
to understanding a few basic things

I have learned a little about purpose,
like why it is
a person would write a poem
that contains the word "myself"

or what it is that artists who are
songwriters first and less accomplished singers second
were trying to say
and with their word and idea surges

I put a greater value than ever
on the enthusiasm and excitement of youth
yet I find myself more and more
wanting to recommend from experience

I am also increasingly aware
that consensus in a self-interested world
seldom collects around wisdom
. . . although I usually trust well-rated recipes

in general, I see our collective faults more clearly;
the greatest of them must be
the agreement to write off
the othernatural as nonsense or unknowable

(as if it is our prerogative to disclaim
the gift of life itself,
along with the lesser gifts of an infinity of connections,
planned outcomes, and life-changing motivations)

I realize more than ever how important it is
to remind myself
that I require God's blessing daily
in the work-a-day world

"May the favor of the Lord our God
Rest upon us; establish the
work of our hands for us—
yes, establish the work of our hands."

it is important for me to refer to a list of important things
to avoid being waylaid by
my attraction to the constructs and societies
that siren-call me to the city

I need to remind myself that, in time,
I will place a sharply discounted price
on all man-made locations and orchestrated events,
each determinedly advertising its own importance

with the inevitability of concrete
being broken over time by humble weeds
pride in our temporary possession of God's, now soiled, globe
will crack and then give way

an older friend assured me
that I will, in time, learn (re-learn)
the unsurpassed attractiveness
of nature's beauty—the original organic produce

another mentor described
how the Great desire grows quiet with accumulating years,
though its diminishing echo
can always be heard

I dreamt
(old men have dreams, or is it visions?)
about the romance between
a young man and a young woman I didn't know

they were unable to comprehend
(but I, the omniscient observer/author, understood)
the dynamics of their first meeting,
and the future that awaited them

the dream was but play-acting,
as my unconscious
spooled out the narrative,
like a controlling Greek god of old

on waking,
my memory of the dream
was mixed with thoughts about the wide gaps
between the few things I can explain

perhaps the best example,
like a higher concept in math I will never understand,
is my inability to comprehend
more than bits and pieces of what it is I long for

jackhammer Christmas

imagine each white Christmas
as a pearl . . .
now hold
the jewel very still

so you can jackhammer
to its centre
and remove
the core

that's what we do when
we banish
Christ's birth
from this most hallowed holiday

and replace
Merry Christmas
with
Happy Holidays

talk all you want
about
the magic
of the season

the real magic of Christmas,
so to speak,
is the
othernatural

trace all giving
far enough back
and you'll see
a babe in swaddling clothes

look at any tree
long enough
and you'll see a Christmas tree
of life

if the words "fall on your knees"
make you cry
you can be sure
you have worshiped

drilling out
the core of the celebration
will, of course,
ruin everything

as we will have to rely
on molded red and white plastic forms
from offshore factories
to inspire us

the giving
no less real (unreal)
than a cash giveaway
at a life-sucking casino

the songs
bland, unaffecting
and the Christmas tree
of knowledge of good and evil

yet, after much conferring
we decided to jackhammer Christmas
in order to better celebrate
the Happy Holidays

Jones, Smith and me

Prayer would be irrational if you didn't believe there was a God who could become involved in your personal affairs. Accepting this as the test, my experience is that prayer is a perfectly rational response. In addition to innumerable more nuanced examples, three striking incidents come to mind, two of which involved one of my brothers.

I once had a longstanding problem with a client I will call Mr. Jones. While the problem was ongoing I met with one of my brothers for a coffee. In the course of our conversation I related my side of the Jones story to my brother. At the end of our meeting I drove my brother to drop him off at the home where he was staying. He asked if he could say a prayer about my situation.

My brother sat in the passenger side of my car and prayed a prayer that matched in intensity the most dramatic moments in the "Lord of the Rings" movie trilogy. He began by describing me to God as a man who was doing his best to honour God. He then prayed that God would recognize this by intervening on my behalf to remedy my conflict with Mr. Jones.

I don't remember the exact phrases—other than he asked God to do anything that was necessary—but I doubt I will ever forget the intensity of my brother's emotion and his serious tone throughout. The prayer was rendered that much more powerful by the setting. It was a stormy night, and waves of the heavy rain were highlighted whenever there was lightning, which seemed to strike at key moments in the petition.

Nothing happened the next day, but in the morning of the second day after I received an unexpected phone call informing me that Mr. Jones had had a dramatic health reversal that was totally unexpected. I immediately felt sick thinking about the prayer of just 36 hours before. Although Mr. Jones' situation was very serious, he fully recovered. As for the conflict, between us, it was immediately resolved.

The second incident was eerily similar in that it involved the same brother. My brother and I speak by phone every week or so. That week we spoke around 9:00 a.m. on a weekday morning. My brother asked how I was doing. I said on most levels I was doing great; however, at that very moment I was feeling empty because for some reason I felt I needed more purpose, needed to do more good: more to help individuals and more for the general community. My brother tried to reassure me by saying that as far as he could tell I was doing lots of good. We ended the phone call shortly thereafter.

Three hours later, I was about to break for lunch when I heard a client come into the office. I recognized the voice as that of a man for whom I had worked for several years. The first time I met the man, let's call him Mr. Smith, he was buying a nice house on acreage with his wife. I remember having thoughts about how I, although older, would likely never be able to buy such a nice property. Another early memory I had of Mr. Smith was that he had won a significant prize in a major contest—another lucky break! Mr. Smith was a big man with the strong build of a rugby player. I would have guessed when I first met him he was around 230 pounds.

When the economy rocketed down Mr. Smith's business was hit particularly hard. So hard in fact that he was unable to make payments to his business creditors, or even make the payments on his house mortgage. I later learned that it was only with the help of family were the Smiths able to pay for the basics of life.

Mr. Smith had been devastated by the reversal. He stopped trying to work; he stopped meeting with people, me included; and he even stopped answering the telephone and replying to emails. His wife later told me that he couldn't eat or sleep, and would often sit as his desk at home for hours, doing nothing. When I saw Mr. Smith just prior to his decision to go bankrupt he looked like a man with AIDS, he walked awkwardly, and my guess is he was around 160 pounds. He avoided looking at me when we talked.

Mr. Smith's wife, God bless her, had no choice but to make all of the economic decisions on her own and do whatever was necessary to keep their family together. Through friends, prayer, and circumstances the business was wound down, the house was sold, and the family was ready to re-start.

And now, some months after the completion of the house sale, Mr. Smith had apparently come by to see me. I walked out to meet him in the waiting room. The first thing I noticed was how much better he looked. My guess is that in the intervening months he had regained twenty pounds, and now had some colour in his face. He looked me in the eye and shook my hand—something he hadn't done for several meetings. As we walked to my desk he told me that he had just stopped by to thank me.

We sat down and Mr. Smith asked me if I could remember when I had made him two lists, one listing his faith, his wife, his kids and other family; and the second listing his business holdings, other assets and his income. I told him I couldn't remember making the lists. He said maybe I would remember if he reminded me how I had taken the second list, torn it up, and thrown the pieces in the garbage saying that there was nothing important on that list. I told him I still couldn't remember the lists. He said that thinking about those two lists had helped him keep going during the past year.

I was overcome with emotion when he said this. Unable to speak, I wrote down a few sentences on a notepad describing my conversation with my brother just hours earlier that day. Mr. Smith asked if he could have the note and I nodded yes. He folded the note up and put it in his pocket. He then went on to tell me how he had learned so much through this, the most difficult time of his life, especially the need to trust God. He asked if he could keep in touch with me in the future, and I said that I would appreciate that.

When he was leaving he turned back to say happily that he had gotten a job. My instant thought was he must have found a job that would help him rebuild his family's finances. Instead, he proudly related that he was going to work for a charitable organization at an out of the way location in another province.

When Mr. Smith left I called my brother back right away. I told him there had been a really weird development. He immediately asked, "How did God show you?" I told him about Mr. Smith's visit to my office. My brother laughed and said that in case I had missed what was going on, earlier in the day he had received an email asking him to speak at a charitable organization at an out of the way location in another province, and although he hadn't paid much attention he was ninety-nine percent sure it was the same one Mr. Smith had just told me about . . . .

The third incident involved me and the medical profession. For as long as I remember I have had two noticeable moles on my neck, one at my hairline. Every year or two for my entire adult life my mother has pressed me to deal with these moles, reminding me each and every time that they might represent something more serious.

One Tuesday I was shaving, and in the rush of the morning I somehow managed to nick one of the moles. It bled profusely and I said to my wife that I was motivated to arrange to have the moles removed. Naively, I set out on the internet thinking that there might be a physician in our overstressed, public medical system who would be available to quickly deal with my problem, which of course there wasn't. I reported back to my wife and said I would have to revert back to the standard procedure of setting an appointment with a general practitioner and getting a referral to a specialist. My wife made the unexpected suggestion that I pray about the situation.

That Saturday, or four days later, my wife and I attended a 50th birthday party. There was a range of vocations represented in the gathering, including several physicians whom I had met once or twice before. Needless to say I did not bring up my mole problem in conversation.

The Tuesday following, now one week after my shaving incident, there was a message on my answering machine at work from one of the doctors. In a very apologetic tone he explained that he had noticed the mole on my neck, and he wanted me to know that if I ever wanted to have the mole removed he would be happy to help out. He said that he happened to be an ear, nose and throat surgeon who regularly dealt with skin abnormalities. He left me his work number, his home number and his cell number.

I was overwhelmed with the timing and content of the message. In our public medical system general practitioners don't phone you, you phone them. As for surgeons, well, they are far less accessible still. Of course, I returned the surgeon's telephone call right away, and he removed the moles later that same week.

Looking back, I suppose the surgeon may have noticed the mole because I had nicked it several days earlier. That said, I believe I had once again been given the gift of seeing God at work, which is like seeing God.

better than David

because I was older
he asked me to comment
on the sort of future he could expect,
so I gave him my best prediction

I said that if his life developed
like mine had
he could expect to encounter
both great highs and great lows

he replied with a wry grin
that our theologies
appeared to be
somewhat different

by which I understood
him to mean that he
anticipated more pervasive joy
and a general protection from setbacks

over the next day or so
I was aware that
at the edge of my thoughts
I was turning over his reply

the kneading process
was to try and decide if he was right
and if my attitude has
been faulty, life-long

eventually, out there,
at the edge,
a decision that satisfied me
was shaped

I decided that my younger friend
was likely too optimistic
since none of us should expect
a better life than David

we know this much
from those of the Psalms
that are attributed to David,
a shepherd, a hero, a king

we know that
David loved God,
God loved David,
and still David suffered, a lot

meaningful

as I sat through a debate
about whether or not religion is beneficial
I circled in on what
I think changes when you believe

first, your circumstances change,
at least in part, and by that
I mean your health,
your wealth and your relationships

the changes are for the better
in some ways, but
some things often go in reverse,
like cash in the bank

change occurs
because your choices
are measured against new values,
although you sometimes slip back

you start to participate in
a new economy
where what was valuable before
is less so now

in this economy
giving to others
is typically far more important than
adding to your savings

in this economy
keeping fit is ranked behind
visiting a friend you haven't seen for a while,
or even someone you don't know that well

when you acknowledge God
everything that happens is meaningful
and nothing that happens
is without meaning

now and then I wonder how
much influence the Bible
had on the drafting of the
Rights of Man

who can deny the imprint
of the the original proclamation of rights,
Christ's message of equality
—equal in sin and redemption

unstable platforms

experience becomes focus
becomes wisdom;
so it is that we become better and better
at describing what we see and feel

at a certain age,
with experience and education,
we become the exact right person to describe
the events we have witnessed

the story-telling ability
of each of us who has lived for long enough
was at the fore at the funeral
of a well-loved man

the in memoriam given that day
by average (brilliantly average?) people
measured out with precision
the qualities of a man no longer with us

. . .

I think regularly on the interplay
between coalescing wisdom and
the decisions made by several of our dear friends,
all about the age of fifty, to leave their spouses

what makes so many move on?
the overriding call of biology;
seeing things more clearly; or
something else entirely?

if breaking your vows results from a physical imperative,
it may be because each relationship,
like with chemical bonding, exhibits
a different level of attraction

if it is an assessment
of the cost-benefit analysis of the union,
knowing how many years are left
will, of course, affect the decision

in more than one debriefing
half (sometimes both) the dividing pair
identified a lack of respect,
one way or the other

in some cases, maybe it just takes years
to build up the courage
to abandon a project
that was always doomed to failure

. . .

we are unstable platforms

. . .

I have jokingly said at times to blame it all on us men:
we grow up funny-like, in stops and starts,
and five decades on
we still laugh at the same few stupid jokes!

. . .

given our self-doubt and proclivities,
we're walking across a floor of teacup saucers anyways;
and then someone takes haunt shots at our feet
from a hundred years in the past

. . .

without a good explanation
for the impasse of personalities
I can but offer myself the thought:
grains of sand in the glorious

what I can't explain

I now accept that writing is
just a
structured way to talk to
myself.

Today I write to document
some things
I cannot possibly
explain.

I should start with a puzzle like:
I know
that you know that I know that
you know;

or . . . the shadow of (not cast by)
the light;
or . . . a crowded life that's
lonely.

I was lonely watching t.v.
last night
until the spark of the
report . . .

. . . our student-poor son had fronted
money
with little thought to its
return.

And I was lonely driving with our
daughter.
Although she talked I was
quiet.

Bizarrely, I was unable to choose
between
my simple and eager
thoughts, like:

how are you . . . and . . . today is
your day
(two of many I left
unsaid).

So, instead I was silently
awkward.
And certain I'll never
know why . . .

. . . I couldn't fix this memory
despite
my having so many
chances.

it wasn't a plane

for much of my life
I have focused on percentages:
49% to fail, 50% to pass, and 80% to 90% for an A.
I've now lived 50 out of 70 years . . .

. . . (the age of 70 being when my dental bridge is
expected to expire) 50/70 or 71%;
according to the math, I have already lived
a strong C, and maybe a C+

which means that
I am now into what would have been
bonus territory for many people from history,
including some I've known

someone please shake me
until I am sufficiently grateful for the day to day
regardless of whether or not I'm embarking
on something new or returning to something old

as I age, I pray I will be more accepting of setbacks
and come to understand that the bushes
that surround me are not meant to narrow my path,
but to keep me on the path

. . .

I already believe chance and planning
couldn't by themselves overcome my tiredness
and guide us 60 kilometres down a small road at night
to where my son's friends were

I also believe technologically admirable,
carefully maintained planes
didn't bring my youngest daughter
home from France

defiling not so modern constructs

both prosperity theology
and the Social Gospel
are, when taken far enough,
unsupportable concepts

neither of them is the Good News
and neither is centered solely
on belief in
the deity of Christ

first, the easy one,
prosperity theology, which in extremis,
wrongly seems to assume that
there should be no judgment ever, of self

defiling
the idea that God will
exclusively bless believers
is accomplished without effort:

"He causes his sun to rise
on the evil and the good,
and sends rain on the
righteous and the unrighteous."

the Social Gospel is trickier.
it properly discharges judgment of the poor,
but it seems determined to promote the judgment
of those who do not appear to want financially

contrast Christ's social gospel
"Do not judge,
or you too
will be judged."

these words
need no comment
and are followed by the strong recommendation
to remove the many planks in our own eyes

I once heard Matthew 5:7
used almost exclusively to indict
those with
any apparent material advantage

                              interestingly, the passage
                              reads, "Blessed are
                              the merciful,
              for they will be shown mercy."

the message included the following musings:
that sexual immorality
may be a lesser sin than
the accumulation of wealth

that misleading
a rule-bound bureaucrat
may be okay if done
to gain protection for the disadvantaged,

and the beguiling idea that the best life
is without question a simple life where
all material advance is carefully leveled
and people live in close community

(granted, there were passing references
to our need to do our best,
and the opportunity for spiritual gain
from setbacks)

while each of these examples
struck me as potentially correct,
they all seemed subject to
an unbearable number of qualifications

my reading of the passage
is that we are to show mercy to . . . everyone,
again, everyone, which has nothing to do with
a rich man, poor man thesis

yes, Christ made it crystal, crystal clear
that feeding the hungry and clothing the needy
is to do the same for him
a thousand times: of course!

and when choosing which master to serve
the self-centered distractions
that come with success and wealth
regularly prove fatal

but mustn't each of us,
for ourselves, decide how
to house our families, and how
best to help out those less fortunate

Christianity
is emphatically not about wealth, or the lack of it,
and Matthew 5:7
is not only for those in a specialized margin

we are all in one predicament or another
(displaced from Eden, we all fall short)
Christianity is about our hearts, and
who can know another man's heart?

> "Working with convicts I can tell you
> that many of them understand something
> the rest of us seem to have missed, which is
> that something inside them is broken."

perhaps the man with investments
is mid-stride in the act of great giving,
and maybe the stressed, white collar woman is taking
the best possible steps to raise educated, Christian children

at our church we once watched
a video showing
the back of a beggar;
people walked by without appearing to notice him

my wife's comment about the video
was that while no one could miss the obvious point
her heart also inclined to
the hard lives of those walking by

then there were hardly any

they're talking again
about the end of oil
but I'm thinking
worse shortages are looming

I fear losing my sense of what's real
working as I do in the virtual:
recently, I weirdly realized
that I could see trees in High Definition

I'm confident I'll get by
without the full range of milk products,
including skim, whole, non-fat,
lactose free and goat

I am worried, though, that
rock stars and their fans are no longer young,
and that there seem to be fewer children
(maybe these things are related)

the decision to truck
fewer strawberries to us in the snow
is a development that
just seems to make sense

but why are people telling me
morality was always a fiction
and the best we can do
is reconfigure the trolley problem

we might be better off
if we were in Europe,
which at least has
innumerable, awe-inspiring, . . .

. . . though poorly attended, cathedrals
that stand in silent homage
to the thought that nothing we do
is ever done in secret

I am unsettled by the decision,
too many editorials wide,
to write little or nothing about
the oxygen lines to society:

Girl Guides and Boy Scouts,
Sunday School,
old folks homes,
Thanksgiving dinner with the family . . .

. . . the charities and missions
in the inner city—I guess the press
can't afford to linger
on the side of the street the church is on

I have some understanding of the trend
to humanize/get rid of
our heroes, our idea men and
even those that sacrificed their lives

just never, ever try to tell me God is gone
and I'm alone
when I'm looking up at the sky
or down on a sleeping child

a telescope

I continue to have
a pronounced difficulty of late
describing the world
in a line or two

however, while searching for
the grand unified metaphor
I have stumbled on
a lesser truth

which is: as you age you begin
to see things both before
and after, the present time.
take a pretty face

now when I see a pretty face
I see its angelic aspect when young,
how it will look in time; and
even a ghosting of each parent's face

this developing power
to telescope the past in (like in Facebook)
and the future out isn't limited to faces,
which, upon study, all turn out to be eerily similar

it applies to objects like trees and buildings
and even sometimes to
the amorphous,
such as politics and culture

there are real complications, though,
when I try to focus on both
the origins and the outcomes
of the choices people make

writing scared

two of the poles
that orient me are
stripped down to written truth, and
not taking my foot off the accelerator

although I have my own understanding
of the world of civilities,
hale fellow
and that sort of thing

when I have time to
ponder on what matters most
I turn away from fiction
and what in fiction proves unnecessary . . .

. . . it seems to me that setting and character,
although traditionally key elements in fiction,
are often there
because they are easier to write . . .

. . . how often have I (and you)
skipped full pages that the author
labored over as I chase the plot,
wanting to find out what happens next;

and I turn towards the fumbling truth of poetry,
where a highlighted word or phrase
is but a fraction as distracting as a subplot,
or a lengthy scientific description

poets don't have the space (or time)
to pad around becoming self-conscious
even less so now that rhymes are acknowledged
to be circus mirrors to meaning

my fear of slowing down
pulls on me differently of course
as it causes me to race ever-faster in public
and friendlessly in private

one consequence of living
in my pell mell world has been
that the people I deal with have lost standing
in the metaphoric animal kingdom

in the constantly lean and mean times
I no longer see people as upright tigers, instead
I see us all as far simpler,
single-celled protozoa

organisms whose motivations
are like a few constituent parts
visible as on a slide, and
oh so easy to catalogue

relationship bomb

Boom!

I love you, we love you

how should people respond, now, years from now

primary cause(s) and catalyst(s)

do/can people change

marriage and God

   loving God and laying down your life for others

whence joy—a life well lived

   pursuit of happiness versus love of others, family, community

cost to you

who else gets hurt

   have you been an example to someone

   generational

who is your confident today

should you seek the opinions of others

can anyone see the future

living alone

meeting someone new

   what problems then

in just 3 days

the irrepressible human spirit
it can be down . . . crushed, really
but it rebounds quite quickly
and is almost okay two days later

and by the third day
you are fully back and able to announce,
at morning's break,
today is going to be a great day

"it took courage to emigrate"
no doubt; and if you think on it
the relentless challenge of life
is the most worthy chestnut of all

so,
I celebrate the human spirit
and, if I had the authority,
I would bless it, and you

the way I see it
the human spirit
is the actor on each of the infinite occasions
we exercise our free will

God guides us, God protects us,
but we must choose
to accept direction,
which means on some days, to just get going

I can cover six sides of this circle,
but not all of it
I hesitate to say that I, for one,
have almost always done my best

looking around, though,
I can say without hesitation
many people I've chanced to meet have done far more
than was expected of them

blessed to have been a witness
I toast my fellow travelers (as at a birthday)
going forward refreshed on day three I say,
today is going to be a great day!

wildwind, fearzone

buffet as you wont, wildwind
but you're too late
I've already hired out to cut down
the suburb-risking giant

through this glass starkly,
sealed and on the 2nd floor,
the mute and patched blue sky
misleads to thoughts of quiet and calm

but violent the wildwind must be
because on closer study the shrubs and small trees
are screaming and jerking about
at a heightened pace

—I didn't even notice the small,
green leaves at first;
who would have thought that leaves
could blow around in May like in fall—

hit with a wave of wind-sea-sickness
I turn back to peer long-ways at some text,
hoping to moor to something
not subject to nature's swells;

and I think on how I could be looking down
on my fearzone, which may seem silent,
but on careful observation
the impact of the storm is obvious

talking about God

The grand intersection
of free will is the question
whether or not we believe.

I asked a friend,
"how do you engage
someone who seems, to you at least,
hell-bent on unqualified freedom?"

after a disclaimer, he said:
" . . . anyways here goes: I don't waste time
on the smaller stuff, which includes
almost all the grey areas"

"I say to the person I'm talking to
there must be a God or else our lives are futile—
it's not unusual for
the conversation to end there"

"if we get past that,
the next thing
I do is ask about their life
and suggest they are inclined seek God"

"I point out that
every self-actualization book,
course, and process
is an attempt to reach out to a greater power"

"but the problem is
on our own we can't
even begin to communicate
with a perfectly just, all powerful God"

"it's then I bring up the history
of the man-God, Jesus
do they know who He was?
do they know what He stood for?"

"I conclude by saying
that while we can't reach
God on our own,
Jesus has connected the infinite divide"

someone reading
my summary cannot possibly sense
the full power
of my friend's delivery;

but I valued each word he spoke
because I know him so well, and
because I use him as a measure
for the amount of love I should have for others

my friend also pointed out
that the people who chose
to talk to him
are usually suffering a setback

and, if you think on it,
if there was no fear, no pain, no death
would any of us even talk about
God?

interestingly, my reading is that
the first time Adam talks to God
(as versus God to Adam)
is after it all goes wrong

that's all

I had stopped the pipe
thinking that I was done writing;
but whatever it is I write
wasn't done with me

there were burbling thoughts
about no fault divorce
as a marker along the way
for so many of my friends

a marker, perhaps,
of a more general breakdown
as we swarm like locusts
to the all-satisfying city

cities were once a part of the whole
where you could find refuge,
but they are much louder now,
and stand apart

the reasons for divorce
have always been the same,
but in the cases I know (all cases?)
at absolute best you can understand one-half

years later while driving
he thought back
and slammed the steering wheel,
angry about what that had happened

fair enough: all wrongs
are built on other wrongs
but somewhere along that sort of scale
nothing we do is all that wrong

which I can't accept:
we're not just endlessly climbing
over one another in a slimy pit
with first you, then me, closer to the air

my experience tells me
that some acts
are clearly wrong
as someone has been made to suffer

. . .

I met an older couple
who had fostered and
then adopted four drug babies,
all of whom later turned to crime

the husband explained
that their children
had each done well until, one by one,
they were re-introduced to drugs

and, in turn, each child stole from them
and hurt them, even physically;
each child apparently unable or unwilling
to recognize his or her own meanness

as gently as I could
I asked the couple what they had learned
from raising children
who had been born without consciences

I was shocked with the man's answer:
he said he had come to realize
that his children were not
that dissimilar from him . . .

. . . as he was often not 100% truthful
and sometimes chose
to benefit himself rather than
to benefit to others . . .

. . . he said, "Back to the question,
the most important thing
I have learned from raising my children is
the depth of the grace God has shown me"

. . .

burbling too
were thoughts about
so many news items
appear to have been chosen for affect

not because they report unusual developments,
but rather because they are
an attempt to direct us
to a common view (. . . whose view?)

not unlike the stories we purposely let
our own children overhear
about some other young person
who has been harmed by his decisions

                    I remember
          confronting one of my children
          with the surprisingly short list
                of the sins you can commit

          and summarizing how these sins, when first met,
                seem to have thrilling personalities,
                        but how in time
                each disappoints or injures

the problem is the parents in this case,
the news editors,
are the same parents
who let their children scream in stores

while some uncontrolled children
gain confidence and independence
I have too often seen
the harm done by willful children

just once I'd love to read a newspaper column
on the calming effect of a message
about turning the other cheek
that hundreds heard in church last Sunday

. . .

unrelated,
were my forming thoughts on health
and the expectations imposed
on the caregivers engaged to help us, somehow

and how, really,
after the first half-century or so
health becomes almost
pure demographics

but a stalk in a wheat field growing older;
instead of always wanting more life
in time I need to simply bless
the new fields down the valley

. . .

burbling . . . burbling
were thoughts about how
I have learned you feel only a limited connection
to grown children

although yours by blood, bone and indescribable love,
they don't feel like an extension of you:
they have left your small spot on the hillside
and have entered the wider stream

. . .

and about how
when I am most in danger
I turn, almost without thinking, to prayer
and worship music

subconsciously I am aware I need
these standards nearby when I face challenges
because they remind me
where my help comes from

. . .

and then, randomly, one night
while driving through the city
and worrying about whatever
was on my mind . . .

. . . it could have been earth-bound asteroids,
viruses, the bomb, climate change,
finite resources, fanaticism, birth rates,
or something else . . .

. . . my wife quoted Romans 8:38 and 39
to remind me of the protections
provided by
the Creator:

"For I am convinced that neither
death nor life, neither angels nor demons,
neither the present nor the future,
nor any powers,

neither height nor depth, nor anything else
in all creation, will be able to
separate us from the love of God
that is in Christ Jesus our Lord."

the exact right day

the most storied emotion
is the variety of love
we call love at first sight,
and most sights thereafter

less important by far, but still
a joyful, unexplained part of my life
are the attachments I feel for
certain inanimate things I own

it turns out
several things I own
are right there,
right there in some sort of special, sweet spot

(like the world's most famous porridge,
these things
are not too much this or that
but are just right)

I recently acquired
an automatic watch
that eliminates batteries,
including their disposal

my one and only gun is perfect,
all wood, all metal,
all tradition, and
smooth lever action

a better example yet
is my old style, mainly steel, carbed,
two-banger motorcyle;
Plato's ideal bike

similarly,
the shape of a '65 Mustang
pleasantly twists me whenever I see it
though I can't explain why

and I am inexplicably buoyed
by the precise colour of blue
of the pair of jeans I wore on my first
day of school, now close to fifty years ago

the most complete pleasure, though,
is a rare happiness that,
almost overwhelms me
on the exact right day

on the exact right day
I feel an immeasurable love
towards all things,
especially living things

beauty can be truth

poetry isn't any good
when you're weighing your options
about making a choice
that you have already made

it's even less useful
when you're in a fight,
with so much at stake,
everything happening so fast

there are no thoughts of poetry
when you're near her face
and think you can see into her emotions,
although you may write it down later

poetry is useful, though,
when you need to go
from where you are
to where you sense you should be

it can help explain why
on a tumbling, swirling day
the best thing you can do
is phone up your oldest friend, . . .

. . . which might be when a grand love
becomes unstayed
or you are suddenly not convinced
by the goodwill of people uptown

and poetry can help you understand
that beauty is only truth when it teaches
you something. That's what I learned
when I was searching for good.

there will be a tomorrow

SONGS AND POEMS TO 2006

road trip

on a road trip, another joke about the rust on the door
on a road trip, you've got the radio and there's tapes on the floor
even though it's just starting you know that it's what you missed
heading into the cool night air on another road trip

tire tracks on Rats and Snakes in this American-made year
boys will be boys when they don't look when they can leer
a long term investment is just a tuxedo on a bet
if it's a mile further on down the road we haven't been there yet

like the moving picture map from "Indiana Jones"
are those your shoelaces and what shoes do you own
signs show on the window, but don't wait before they go
someone said something and you wonder how he knows

no one does their income tax on the road out of town
by Sunday night it will all be coming down
trash the mid-day project and burn commitment to the ground
Billy hasn't called back yet but he'll come around

motorcycles and marriage

Motorcycles have helped me understand marriage.
When I bought my motorcycle
I really didn't know what I was getting into.
Who could have guessed at the cost of insurance,
the problems I would encounter storing the bike, or
even the quandary of when and where to drive.

I felt an immediate and resolute allegiance
to my new motorcycle, and I always think of it with affection.
I bought it for good reasons, of course, including
the thrills that accompany acceleration, speed, and leaning into a curve;
the possibility of trips full of adventure to distant places; and
the connection between my motorcycle and the great motorcycle ideal.

It turns out, though, that one motorcycle is not enough.
Sure, this one may be fuel efficient with a wide band of torque,
but it lacks the raw horsepower to do a quarter mile in under 13 seconds,
and I fear it cannot do the tonne.
I have been looking at a European sport bike with a sixties heritage,
but the problem is that I can only afford one wife.

here's to you

here's to you
may all your ambitions stay healthy
and your strong suits remain
here's to you
may your faith be secure
until your dying day

each kiss is imbued with a long history
the first marks of grey were so hard to believe
an unfinished list of the better outtakes
never forgetting life's whatever you make

a smile that arrives after traveling for years
and then words that calm the re-surfacing tears
winning shots in a game where no one keeps score
something else on your mind but you thank them once more

a look of love that seems never to change
Da Vinci might have left the ground with this art
a note of sadness that can never be feigned
all the way round and then renewed at the start

a poem can't say

A poem can't say
more than the
poet is
able to say.

Poems aren't alive,
though, words stare,
signal, and
even survive.

Poems, you will find,
describe scenes,
random thoughts,
and life most times.

A poem can't hide:
our beliefs;
who we love;
the reasons why.

Poems come of age
when images
exceed the
poem and page.

Still, poems can't say
more than the
poet is
able to say.

real life

life, the uncertainty of real life
no two minutes are at all alike
there something wrong can turn our all right
or you can die a slow death from a mosquito bite

I don't take in too much oxygen—that drug's too hard on me
breathing in and out I'm not promoting ozone therapy
I don't take too much oxygen—its affects I can't explain
even just a little keeps me coming back again

I don't ask my own opinions on too many tricky things
when it's late in the evening I'll tell you what the morning brings
I don't ask my own opinion about some old guarantee
that rambles on and on about happiness and liberty

I don't take many pictures and make a cult of some event
why should I have a thousand thoughts about what it is something meant
I don't take many pictures—the past has mainly lost its use
although I admit that when I see my wife I see the wife of my youth

education kills

education kills the young
it erodes a person's reliance on things not seen
until he only trusts
what he can see and what he hopes to learn

education is a cautious parasite
waiting at least one generation
before it brings about its own demise
by killing the children of its host

they say that everybody needs
"a good liberal education"
and who wouldn't think that
education is the very best thing

back in the beginning we needed to learn
how to stay warm
how to grow food
how to protect ourselves

children need education to become adults
adults need education to advance
education is the source of language
and the medium of culture

but farther along the path we are on,
where we find all of this good, and more where it came from,
we will come upon the unyielding truth
that knowledge remains a mix of good and evil

oh, tree of knowledge,
so dichotomous in ambition,
a sign directing us first this way, and,
then directing us the other way

science is good, then it mined asbestos and mercury
science is good, then we became so
engine-powered that we killed every single fish
science is good, then came eugenics in its many disguises

science is good, then it helped us build cities
where early morning deliveries allow us to forget
the farms, the weather, the seasons, and
our reliance on the great mysteries

"Don't worry. Science will yet make
this earth a wonderful place to live."
What?
What about the bomb that will never go away?

that said, education didn't even need the bomb
to kill the young
it only needed to turn us sufficiently inward—
the instrument of death a solipsistic spiral

since there is nothing beyond
what we have learned
and what we hope to some day learn
there is little else that we need

we don't need help from others
we don't need families
and we certainly don't need children—
in fact, we won't have any children

buffalo gal

buffalo gal
I'm in the City and its getting late
seems the new millennium has got me in its wake
I'm not sure who to trust or what rules apply
only you can laugh with me without needing to ask why

my memories are on their own
—I seldom check to see what's gone
just images of you stay on
when all the rest are sifted through
there is no hype and yet it's true
I'm always thinking about you

then someone said, "around the world,
odds on we won't be back again"
this time it was an idle threat,
a tour of duty I won't do
you see, the days drag on so long
whenever I'm away from you

the faint outline of someone's soul
is sketched by the stories they choose to tell
while listening you're always on my mind
it's like you're there and you'll hear too
because no story ever ends
until its been retold to you

ode to little Mer-Mer

It is one thing to be,
to be beautiful, smart, and . . .
It is another thing to do,
to do something so well that, from one perspective at least,
it seems to have been done perfectly.
(To be fair, this prose poem from a father to his daughter
could be written by any parent about an athletic child.
The names, the plays and maybe the sport would change,
but the subjective pride would be the same.
You should hear me describe the way Peter runs,
or uncle Rodd go on and on about Dawson.)

You started your new role as sweeper
– its hard to believe now that you once played up –
when coach Bill sensed we could lose the Calgary game.
You asked me what you should do,
and the only answer I could give you
was that you knew the position better than anyone,
certainly better than I did.
After your collision with Calgary's speedy forward on the first play,
there were no more threatening runs into our end.
Like every forward since then
she must have realized that you do not yield, ever.

We will always remember your collision with Alanna K,
as the soccer season approached Christmas,
when you covered for one of your team mates by intercepting
the charging wing in the nick of time.
The problem was you hadn't seen Alanna K racing up,
and it almost cost you a broken bone
– in fact, one of the parents (a nurse) said that she heard a bone break.
Two hours in emergency confirmed, thank God,
that nothing was broken.
(It turns out the Silver Bullets won the game when Nicole
got the goal she had promised you
while you were laying on the stretcher.)

Your courage in soccer
– and in all other parts of life –
is your greatest strength.
(Mom says your name stands for protector.)
As far as soccer goes,
your second best attribute is your understanding of the game.
You know exactly when to challenge for the ball by
running up into mid-field;
you know exactly when to pass the ball back to your keeper;
you know exactly where the danger lies, and
exactly when you need to move left or right.
These are called intangibles.
With no more advice to give I just watch and cheer.

Your speed, strength, balance and agility
allowed you to seize control of the Chilliwack game
– it may have been the most important game of the year –
by challenging number 3 in mid-field
on the two occasions she had a chance at the ball,
and by running down number 10 in the final minutes of the game,
showing impossible acceleration and timing
as you kicked the ball away from her at the very last possible second.
You willingly paid for your lost footing
with three or four rolls on the hard ground.
(It was after you ran down number 10
that Ali S's grandfather, who knows soccer,
said you were the best sweeper in the league.)

Next up was Abbotsford.
Again, their forwards could not get by you;
and neither could the GEUSC strikers in the game that followed
– in the GEUSC game you wrongly chastised yourself
for the own goal (if you remember anything I have said
remember that an own goal just means
you were in the middle of the play).

In North Van you were ghostly white, with no voice or energy.
The only visible signs of life were your red cheeks,
which shone like two otherworldly orbs –
it was almost like you had consumption.
You did what needed to be done on defence, and somehow
you hit the most magnificent one timer I have ever seen
by a youth on a soccer pitch, boys and girls –
you told me later that the other fullbacks
had been trying to call you off,
thinking that you would miss the ball
and that it would bounce past everyone.
(One of the parents came up to me later,
stared me down until I had become sufficiently serious,
and then told me that only the most gifted of athletes
could have hit the ball in mid-air like you had done.)

The biggest game was Cordova.
Its funny, but I have started to expect so much of you
that I have a hard time appreciating everything you do now.
Other parents told me later that you had saved one,
and maybe even two goals.
I do remember you challenging, shoulder to shoulder,
the striker who later subbed in for goalie on the shootout
– the senior linesman complemented whoever you were on that play as he
walked by our team to stay abreast of the play –
and I remember you challenging a really big girl
who tried a run through the middle.
Now that I think about it,
the play that stands out most for me
wasn't even an important play.
Way off in the far corner
you had leapt in the air to control a ball.
I remember thinking how high and fluid your jump was,
and admiring your ability to direct the ball so accurately.

Of course, it turned out, Cordova was not the biggest game,
there was a bigger one yet: Semiahmoo in the finals.
I don't even know where to begin,
whether to begin
with how you had broken your finger snowboarding,
and how it had to be wired together in two places,
and how the doctor had said that
"Under no circumstances!" were you to play the big game on April 2,
and how mom had refused to come to the game
because you were going against the doctor's orders,
and how she didn't want to see the finger re-injured
and you sent back at Children's Hospital.
I said a prayer before the game,
"God, please keep her safe."
That was all I prayed.
For once I really didn't care how you played
or if the team won.

You started the game slowly,
and every few minutes coach Bill asked
if you wanted to be substituted;
later he told me that to his "delight" you always said no and played on.
You only fell down once in the early going,
trying to land in a way that protected the full splint on your left arm,
but by the time Ali S tied the game
you were back to playing your usual game,
racing this way and that, throwing yourself around,
and generally doing whatever it took
to keep the ball out of our end,
and especially our net.
In case I have forgotten to tell you,
from my perspective you should have been carded
for fouling the girl who had the jump on you
on the right side of the field;
however, I was later assured by several parents
that you had indeed been contesting for the ball
before you and the Semiahmoo player went down hard
in a rolling heap.
This time and every other time you fell,
I yelled out to you, "Are you okay Mer-Mer?"
Each time you responded with a nod.

I don't know which play was your best,
but when you leaped through the crease to knock the ball clear
of what would have been an empty net goal by their striker
the bench erupted with a shout for "Mer-Mer!"
Jaclyn L scored and the Bullets won
– two winning goals in the final three games for your best friend
on the team, way to go Jaclyn L.
Oh yeah, and your finger was still intact.
That game may have been the only time I did not study your performance,
and when it was announced that the four officials
(never before had I seen four adults – head referee, 2 linesman and a
fourth for substitutions – referee a youth game)
had chosen you as the team's MVP I was a little bit confused.
I mean Alanna K had played so well,
and what about Nicole B, and Jaclyn L? And Ali S?
Really, what about any of the other Silver Bullets?
During the team picture you didn't want to hold the MVP trophy,
but you agreed to do so when coach Bill went out of his way to ask you.
A few minutes later coach Bill pulled you aside
to tell you that you were the MVP for the season as well.

On the way home you fell asleep. Walter
– remember, he was the friendly, retired Austrian gentleman who drove
us to the game . . . remember how he told you about breaking his legs and
ankles so many times skiing and ski-jumping in the old country –
anyways Walter looked back and saw you asleep in the back seat.
He smiled and said with a little laugh that it had been a perfect day.

Actually, it had been a perfect season.

soulmates

soulmates, passing in the night
exchanging fresh and new and happenstance
for something old and right

I'd enjoy talking to you—more to you than almost anyone
did you keep what you believed, what has stayed and what has gone
tell me all your hidden thoughts and tell me what you've done

I'd enjoy talking to you—more to you than all the rest
whatever happened to the gang and the few we knew the best
I'll be your confessor figure speaking only on request

I'd enjoy talking to you—I'll get to you somehow
a quiet supper by the sea, light reflecting off your brow
to learn what you've been thinking, and what you're thinking now

cities without pain

naturally we gain
advancement from pain

yet here in the modern West we do not want
to live in the way life should be lived
and we strive to be pain-free,
extending this ambition to its fullest length
we strive to be death-free,
and we fully expect that with enough effort,
our efforts complemented by
the icons of the new religions, namely,
proper sentiment, celebrity pronouncements,
wrist-bands, and whatever object we embrace next,
we will be able to will
a final cure for both pain and death

pain is not wanted here in these parts
and finds itself under attack
by the old, analog weapons used against pain in the past,
cigarettes, booze and pills,
as well as, the new, digital weaponry of
state-protected choices and freedoms,
endless state-funded medical care, and,
of course, updated pills
don't tell me what to do—I want to do it all,
don't let me suffer, and above all
don't let me die (as I am almost certain
that brief moments of spiritual
and philosophical enlightenment
still await me on what I hope
is an ever-softening globe)

it has struck me, though, that
it may not be all that simple
to isolate ourselves from pain—
you know, the syndrome of "be careful what you ask for . . ."
the most primitive example that comes to mind
in regard to the goodness of pain are the setbacks
that we all acknowledge having benefited from,
and the more I think about it
the more complex it appears to be
isn't pain the conjoined twin of boredom—
take away all of the pain and challenge
and you will end up with boredom
not right away, or in equal measure,
but eventually and approximately
isn't this why we find ourselves
combating boredom, with television,
and with sports and pastimes—the burgeoning
interest in card games, and roulette wheels,
and horse races, and slot machines come to mind—
and trips annually to somewhere warm,
and erudite discussions and hollow debates,
some even trying their hand at poetry

pain has always had an important role to play
it kept us from what was hot, and sharp, and bad for us
the irony is that civilization itself is like leprosy
in that our comforts stop us from being alerted
when things that are really going wrong
worst are the sarcophagus, soulless cities
which embolden us into thinking that
there is nothing that can't be built or fixed
. . . I wonder how long it will be until those of us
in the cities notice that the winds are stronger than ever,
the waves are higher than ever, and every natural
migration that ever took place outside these walls has stopped

when you are pain free you have no hopes
no aspirations
there is no reason for permanent or even
direct connections with anyone else
there is no need for family, and for that matter
the more family you have to be concerned about
the greater your chances of feeling pain;
without pain, you are freed from thinking
about everything, except you and your need for
ongoing protection and comfort,
you reasonably conclude that as long as there
are a certain number of "others" around
whatever needs to be done will be done
to keep you in the manner
to which you have become accustomed

you need pain to remember God
I think the message in Christ's words,
"woe to you who laugh now, for you will mourn and weep"
and later "he who is humbled will be exalted"
is that while we may have a natural inclination
to worship the Creator,
in order to love God (and others)
we need to devalue ourselves,
and the problem in a pain-free world
is our lives are so valuable

that it was in me
to leave the city

animals

are we just,
birds whose fancy feathers weigh us down,
bears reaching up a well-clawed tree
are we spiders mating just before we die,
dog's marking everything we see

have you started counting animals
to find out which have gone extinct
or spent time considering the question
of who will be the next to blink

pet store parrots who talk until they're sad
say things that they don't really know
mastodons, wondering how it got so cold,
lay down for a minute in the snow

and who else can sing in harmony
and who else wonders when they'll die
are we just goldfish with circling minds
or should we begin to wonder who we are

a poem isn't

poems used to rhyme, but haven't for a hundred years
rhymes are like the items of clothing
they used to make with whale bones
the same goes for a poem's formal structure
oh sure, you may be able to identify
meter, alliteration and even a set number of lines per verse
but nowadays these characteristics should be as unpredictable
as a melodic bar in free-form jazz
words, ideas and surprises are all a modern poem has

from the first edit until the last (and editing is never really finished)
the poet replaces his original words with the right words
sometimes a big, shiny word surfaces,
sometimes even a foreign phrase,
but rarely should a showstopper be left on the page

a poem should present a big ideal if it can
—and remember, sometimes small is big
love, death and honor are big, but the problem is
most big ideas have been walked over more than our national parks
and there's no one I know who has the time or need
to make a weekly trek up to Lake Louise

the surprise can be in the idea;
layout and metaphor can also shake you up,
with the buzz lingering after the poem's resolution
but for a real shock, forego print for recitation

never missed a meal

should I pay down the mortgage
or provide aid to somewhere else
trade up to a newer car
or send food to Bangladesh
should we worry if our ends meet
should we worry about the bills
when not one of us has ever missed a meal

confused by all the mortgage options
and graphs that show the rising price of land
stunned by declining business prospects
eroding prices and all the rumours that abound

one friend says money is just a scorecard,
it tells him when he is doing well
another says a depression has started,
he stopped buying and now he's trying to sell

am I like the rich you ruler
tell me, are they my neighbours too
and what are the circumstances
when you can turn from those who ask of you

                    *   *   *

am I doing what I want to
am I doing what I should
would it really make a difference
if I was doing what I could

in the ideal

parents love all of their children equally
when they consider each child in the ideal

when they think about a child in the ideal
there is no conflict, or disappointment, past or present

in the ideal
a child is removed from the here and now and can be seen

    climbing the front stairs after a long absence
    or
    sprawled out, fast asleep on the couch after a stretch of
    flat out, no holds barred living,
    or
    intently asking a question about school, work, or, on occasion,
    even life itself

mostly, parents see their children in the ideal

California in 1965

our love is like California in 1965
we kept going west
until we knew we had arrived
reveling in the sun
we crossed the river where it's wide
our love is like California in 1965

California in the present is less than what you see
a coastal bio-mass of one-half of what it should be
the cities aren't uncovered unless there is a breeze
if you go to certain sections you might never leave

when you drive the highway that runs along the coast
old signs by dead streams mark where the salmon come the most
every farmer's crop a new genetic legacy
empty lots are the footprints of retreating industry

it's a hot and crazy route that the tourist all take north
Mickey's out the window; don't they know what he is worth
an unruly vineyard heralded by some grapes of wrath
no new water in the system—you knew it couldn't last

I *could not write a poem*

other writers have exhausted the words I need
words that fit, words of precision
the problem is most of the good words have been overused
and they no longer work as well as they once did

vitality was stolen away from such words as,
"longing", "love", and "ravished"
(there are other words as well)
these words were once in their prime,
some of the best words ever

working back to front on my shortened list,
the end was in sight for the word "ravished"
the moment the first pulp novel hit the stands
poof. fiction did in a formerly robust word
to say that the word "ravished" is now lifeless
is as accurate as
saying that you haven't seen a saber toothed tiger lately

novel writers were mere accomplices
when the original meaning from the word "love"
was sucked out of it, leaving it dried up like a long-dead insect
the kingpins in the cabal were the lyricists
who made sure that every song they ever penned was about love
when I hear the word "love" now
I think of someone else's cold coffee

if you ask a poet for an explanation
about what happened to the word "longing"
be certain he or she will turn away,
and decline to answer

since there so few useful words left
I no longer try to describe the most important things
and that is why
I could not write a poem for you

in faith

God, whose purposes are too out-of-size
(the multiplier bigger than all known numbers)
for us to begin to understand
despite our puny declarations to the contrary

created—a word that seems totally inadequate—
a universe of more than infinite proportions
in zero time using zero effort,
a mere God-thought

amazing to think that
into this endless spacescape
all living things were thought into being,
including, it goes without saying, our ancestors

who, we are told,
were made in God's image—
except presumably their human forms—
and, as a result, given the greatest freedoms

which freedoms they immediately used
to disobey the one and only rule,
and set out on the earth-bound part of their sojourns
without consideration for their God

this disobedience was caused by a selfishness
(my physical and other concerns and what I think I understand)
that was more compelling, seemed more real,
at least in the first instance, than anything else, even God

upon reflection, selfishness
is perhaps a product of the interests and inclinations
of our ancestor's human forms,
forms which, by the way, they quickly learned to clothe

the problem is that,
like pet dogs who have tasted fresh blood,
our ancestor's choice for self proved irreversible
for them and every generation that follows

yet, God was (and remains) always there
and all things in his Creation—
every item being marked by His design—
summon each generation to worship

it turns out that the true purpose of Creation
is worship of the Creator, and it turns out
that the harmony provided in this form of worship
provides the greatest peace

but even though they were drawn to God
our ancestors found themselves unable to now access God
because their historical and present disobedience
so offended His God-holiness

in response He, to begin with, offered
access to Himself through
sacrifice and contrite hearts,
especially acknowledgment of Him

later, He authored the divine epic
wherein He physically re-introduced
His very self, in the form of His Son,
to His own Creation

this living story—which cannot be forgotten—
ensured that each person of each generation can,
despite all accumulated disobedience, access God
by believing in His Son (yes, simple belief!)

of course, as earthly matters
approach the edge of God-matters
unsolvable mysteries, too many to count, come into view
like, for example, how three persons make one God

and why did the first man and woman have to be given
the freedom to choose, resulting in centuries of pain
and, for an easier one, how we are to combine
a duty to witness with a duty not to judge

but God knew the limitations of humanity
and so He made (makes) it easy to understand
the central aspect of the God-message,
that is:

His Son died in the great sacrifice
so that those in God's image
who were soiled by ongoing self-interest
could be clothed in the God-holiness of His Son

you would expect this unparalleled news to herald
a celebratory reconciliation
as the created were now given the opportunity
to regain communication with their very Creator

the problem is those in God's image, yet in human form,
are often unable to forego their love of self
in comparison, predators far more readily
let loose the prey they grasp in talon or claw

the reason why it's hard to accuse ourselves and submit to God
is another impenetrable God-matter
despite the darkened glass,
we move forward in faith

stuck on sticks

I'm starting to see too much
it's like I've got x-ray eyes
no matter what they say
it's all coming out like lies

it's like we're all stuck on sticks
twisting around and yet we won't admit
that almost everything is a moral question
the other stuff just feels like its new
don't tell me you're honest or that it's true
I need to know if God's hand is on you

everything is topsy-turvy
I can hardly eat the food they serve me
as the added sugar burns out most things
it's like tasting metal when my bones are sore
now I see frames where I used to see forms
how come I can't trust how I feel anymore

when you're older and your muscles are thin
you realize that cold rocks protect from the wind
that even the young get very tired
that time covers up what deserves more attention
and every editorial yet to be written
should start and end with the Redemption

climate change and natural good

Christianity has caused wars
and all kinds of other problems

I've heard Christians are killing off the last few tigers
and captain the ships that over-fish the seas
I think you can assume that some serial killers are Christians
wasn't Hitler a Christian

if we stop focusing on the great beyond
we'll be able to fix the things that await our ingenuity

once we rid our system of that opiate
we'll make great things, like wine goblets
sure, we'll use lead at first, but we can get past that
then we'll make non-stick cookware
the concerns about those chemicals are exaggerated anyways
we've mastered birth control so we're finished with war

religion is so prejudicial
think about how much love is possible on this planet

look at the love between nations
when religion doesn't rear its ugly head
. . . and when there aren't ethnic cleansing issues,
. . . and when someone's great-someone wasn't killed by someone else;
. . . and when there isn't some old dispute over a piece of land
I guess what I'm saying is, think about the enlightened,
secular societies, you know civilized places—of course,
there'll always be crime and race issues, and morality does change

in my house
we've learned to live without God

we trust each other with the information
we decide the others need to know
blood loyalties run deep here—mind you I never want
to see some of my family members again—
we accept each other's choices
and we even enjoy the gap between generations
although I will never understand why my kids
haven't started families, you know traditional families

don't be fooled into thinking
anything depends on your belief in God

I mean there might be a Supreme Being but so what
I don't claim to know what it's all about, no one does
my hope comes from chance and effort I guess
I'm here for me, well, and my family . . . and I suppose I'm here
to enjoy some things you'll find in my garage
sure climate change matters but I like working on my car

thankfully there's a lot
of natural good in this world

for whatever reason there's pervasive good, I've even got my share
Darwin would probably say life goes better with good
if I'm lucky enough to have someone bother to help me out
at the end of my days . . . well, God bless them

I *believe*

I believe; help me with my unbelief

remembering You when I'm pushed back
to watch my whole world break down
at half-speed in an unpredictable way
it takes time to even accept there's been
a turn for the worse
but unease settles on me after the delay

remembering You when
light dissolves and darkness forms
and the once urgent sounds have
disappeared with the day
I lie awake with nothing else
to keep me preoccupied
except a slender faith much too fragile to convey

*   *   *

I look up and ask Your hand
to come down right away
I want You to touch things
I want You to change things
I want You to make it all okay

Judas's Kiss

Christ,
fully man and fully God.

Manness. Godness.
It struck me that Christ's manness
might have contributed to Judas's decision
to betray Christ.

(The Bible refers to the manipulations of Judas by the evil one,
and I have also considered the direct involvement of God
who sees around and through the consequences of everything.)

A sense of competition,
of motivating envy,
lies between men.
Perhaps this played a role in
the decision by Judas,
to betray, with a kiss,
the One who was
fully man and fully God,
Christ?

saints and killers

Saints and killers were nearby
when I went back in time
to the place where I was raised,
a sometimes mean, distant outpost.

I sat next to a man whom I was drawn to admire
in the course of eating a meal on Christmas eve.
He displayed the physical grace and confidence
of an athlete. He had a reputation for making
good decisions, and had been sought after
to guide his town located in the interior
in the completion of more than one
important civic projects.
His son, who sat with us, was exceedingly
likeable and would have been a credit to any father.

To my surprise, my dinner companion,
got around to telling a story that involved
people I knew from my hometown.
He talked with particular admiration
about a man known to me,
whom he described as skilled, courageous and loyal.
He carried on with additional stories
after I commented, attempting to adopt
a supportive tone, that I had been
raised in the same town as his friend,
and had known his friend
thirty-five years earlier.

The problem was I remembered his friend
as a dissolute and bullying youth, a lout.
His friend, and the family of his friend
had been thought of by me and my friends
as a threat to our day to day lives.
The boys in his friend's family, I think there were only
boys, all wore dirty clothes,
had dirty ambitions, and
were considered by others to be

terrorists in a small town way.
Two of my friends who left
my hometown many years ago
have since described the town
as a place populated by evil people.
I considered the family of my
dinner companion's friend
to be from that group.

I specifically remember the brother
of my dinner companion's friend
leading a gang of grade seven boys
in a self-described game of "booby trap"
that was played with certain
more hardened grade seven girls,
a game which, upon reconsideration,
could only be viewed
as a collective sexual assault.
I also remember regular
incidents when both his friend
and his friend's brother gratuitously
abused a slighter friend of mine
by threatening to strike him,
by actually striking him, and even by choking him—
for the record, the last time
I saw my own friend he was
a loving husband (and a skilled engineer).

I was therefore disoriented as I listened
at the dinner table to stories involving
his friend's bravery and generosity.
I intently studied my companion's remarks
in the hope of identifying a fracture line,
some detail that would confirm
a fatal flaw in the character of
of the storyteller or his subject.

Early on nothing stood out as
obviously off-putting.
Even the brief allusions to excessive
drinking, relationships gone sour, and
humorous deception seemed all too human.

I began to accept that
his friend (my former enemy)
might have changed, or my
memories might be the distorted
memories of a child. I found myself
remembering that his friend's
brother had once invited me over to
their house; and I unearthed
vague memories of
a not unfriendly and knowing mother.

About this time my dinner companion
told a series of unsettling
hunting and fishing stories.
To be fair, only the first two stories
involved his friend. In the first story
he and his friend caught something
over 100 fish out of a modest river,
keeping all of them of course.
The second story involved his friend killing
a large fish off a Mexican tourist coast,
and having it stuffed and mounted.

A story that was not about his friend
involved another man from my hometown who
shot three moose on the same hunting trip
and at the same place—the shooter claiming with a wink
that he thought he was shooting the same animal
over and over again as it kept getting back up.
In the final story my dinner companion related
seeing a picture of so many dead geese
that they were overflowing
the brim of a pickup bed.
I was raised in the north,
and, having hunted and fished (though not well),
neither of these activities fills me with horror.
However, somewhere past
relaxed conservation ideals
there is a type of killing
that is pure blood lust,
and like all of the lusts it is satisfying
to (if only temporarily so), and retold

fondly by, a certain type of man.
I suppose if the stories had originated
far enough back in time
they might be considered examples of
yesteryear's bounty of fish and wildlife,
but this consideration did not apply.

Maybe it is more difficult to
triangulate your conduct with fixed truths
in certain locations and situations.
I know that over the course of our
festive meal I had increasingly
tended towards approving the stories
that were being told with old-boy gusto.
It took effort
—and lessened the cheer of the season—
to identify an observable malfeasance
in the conduct and aspirations
of my companion and his friend.
The dissonance did not clear for
several days, and I will never be sure
if the fault I found was
the fault I had presupposed.

spin me right

please spin me right
because sometimes I don't even know
when I'm out of control
so much is spinning me somewhere else
please spin me on to something pure,
something noble, something to admire
please spin me right

you watch helplessly as your lifelong demons settle down on you
Mister Failure-To-Forgive is not a son of nature
the weak screams of ego warn you to concentrate on something new
the devils murmur back that you should wait until you're sure
by then it's too late because when they're this close they're out of range
from here on in you'll need a miracle to make a change

early in the morning but things have slowed down and the day seems long
it's all old and boring . . . nothing excites you anymore
your birthright for part of the culture, be it right or wrong
by the way forget what's right since you've done all that before
ever wonder why all the thoughts that come from your heart are the
same
from here on in you'll need a miracle to make a change

spelunking

in a poem, while ideas may flop
words will always rise to the top

anybody can be a poet
poets stretch words, then stop
so they can turn them inside out
teop, teop, teop

poets heartlessly steal
names nicked with a child's know-how
which are emphatically wrong but sound real
Dew-Dew, Auntie Bubba and Auntie Wowl

poets seek youth and not fame
since the young know which words to tweak
which of course can't be explained
Molly-Moo, Mer-Mariney and Petey-Weeks

adult poets become convinced
that truth can be described
so they busily look for important hints
about who, how, where and why

they'd be far better off thunking
about words like _____

mother, say a prayer for me

moving and weightless just like the light
reflecting off things, not making a sound
not my world, but the spirit of time
says, "follow me" and shows me around

I'm so alone I could be on a moon of Jupiter
looking out at the wind-swept ground and barren hills so dark
these epic views mean nothing when there's no one around
I'm going to leave when I've got what it takes to start
it gets cold when you think about the giant astral ball
dreaming about a beauty that's so stark
mother, say a prayer for me

on the street I see buildings that reach up and never end
I couldn't build one of them in ten thousand years
elsewhere they are smashing things to study their attraction
it's "strange" and it's "charm" and it's way too small to see
go ahead and manipulate my very DNA
hardly anything would change on earth if I wasn't here
mother, say a prayer for me

a change in the weather can come like a line in the sky
to be touched by God and then to reach to those without names
I realize that I'm staring into the heart of the good
and am reminded that the truth is almost always strange
so many years out and I'm still waiting to engage
any pathways I see now might not be their again
mother, say a prayer for me

are you getting any closer

are your getting any closer
have you decided how to act
who are you going to love
how do you know what is correct
are you getting any closer

it's hard to focus on the epic that's divine
when you're surrounded by the finite, cold and grey
sad stories land on the ground like science fiction rain
you try and see the great beyond but there's so much in the way

it's hard to focus on the epic that's divine
when you can't tell your friends what's really on your mind
attempts to understand your growing isolation
haven't been successful even though you're giving it more time

it's hard to focus on the epic that's divine
when we dilute beauty with every best dressed list
new disasters every day it's so hard to be appalled
you test what looks good and you find out it's a mix

truth in Hosea

People die,
someday you will and someday I.
Still there is truth from God in *Hosea*:

"When I fed them they were satisfied;
when they were satisfied, they became proud;
then they forgot me."
. . . then they forgot me

Suffering's unfair;
conflict is everywhere.
There is a calming truth in *Hosea:*

"For I desire mercy, not sacrifice,
and acknowledgment of God
rather than burnt offerings."
. . . rather than burnt offerings

Anxiety – fear;
meaningless – the end is near.
So I turn to the truth in *Hosea*:

"So you must return to your God;
maintain love and justice,
and wait on your God always."
. . . and wait on your God always

everything

since I don't understand myself
I must have a soul

we want to see greatness
that's all we want
to see what others see and get what we haven't got
how things land and where they roll
is another thing I don't control anymore
another thing I don't control

measure in the mirror
the slow, unsteady gait
first there was a flurry and now you sit and wait
and whatever went before
is another thing I don't control anymore
another thing I don't control

no matter what you say
it's a tricky world
get ready to leave the pool all you boys and girls
who's coming in and going out the door
is another thing I don't control anymore
another thing I don't control

*   *   *

everything is Yours, Lord
and that's all I need to know

infinity

the brazen moth flies to the flame
its very best celebration
is centered on a beauty that decays,
a fanfare of double-speak that promotes
relentless contest, chaos, and death
all the while having to overlook self-interest,
foremost and always self-interest

when I was young but growing older
I learned the super-word "infinity"
a word whose definition was then,
and would always be, beyond my comprehension
because, of course, infinity goes on forever,
and forever is something none of us understand
since our experience is that everything ends

in time my new word,
like all collected knowledge and enjoyments,
was reduced to became merely rote,
the common glaze being applied again and again,
in the case of this new word even while watching cartoons

many years later my, now, old word
was renewed for me
when I read again
Christ's parable of the lost sheep,
this parable, one of the most compelling,
is the story of a lost sheep
who, when lost, apparently becomes
more important than
the other sheep in the flock

the story would seem to make more sense
if the shepherd had taken the flock
to a well-protected pen before abandoning them
to go and find the lost sheep
but in Christ's story
the shepherd decides

to simply leave the flock in "open country"
the idea of risking the lives of many sheep
in order to save the life of one lost sheep
made sense to me only when
I considered the concept of infinity
if each individual sheep was of infinite value,
then, and only then, would the life of one sheep
be worth as much as two, or even ninety-nine sheep,
whether one sheep or many
their value would still be infinite

an inner peace settled on me for a time
when I thought about this message
I, you, we are all apparently invaluable,
whether we are very young, very old,
infirmed—perhaps the lost sheep was sickly—
or, in contrast, even if we are
described, for a time, as exceptional

every current in the unmapped wind
serving open flight
the atmosphere is love
forgetting self,
if only from time to time,
in order to sense the shepherd is near
there will be a tomorrow

othernatural

POEMS TO 2008

the winter of '07

I remember how cold it was
in the Winter of '07,
at the very least it seemed
to get colder, sooner that year

the arrival of the cold
introduced the busyness season
and a developing fear that no activity
would lead to meaningful progress

you know you are too busy
when the things you do blend
into a common, bland mixture,
rendering even the better events repetitive

you know you are getting old
when you realize that,
despite your best caution,
you have been marked by age

you are dented,
scratched, rusty, and dull,
not through and through, but like
an older car someone looked after

you know you are getting old
when you finally understand that
independence means distance
and distance means conflict, yes

you know you are getting old
when you catch yourself
leaning against your porch thinking
rather than continuing to do

(thinking about how love carries forward
for years: love's radioactive background)
even though you know that
what you were doing was probably important

but early on
in the Winter of '07
the thesis, that the world is fundamentally
changed, was almost ready

not changed,
like the difference between
a horse-drawn carriage and
automobile transportation

fundamentally changed,
like the molecular make-up of food,
which looks better than ever
but has no taste

the best ideas we ever had
have been so manipulated that now,
tattered and threadbare, they embarrass
those who wear them

what now passes for great
won't be great later
even though it may have seemed new
. . . the Emperor had more clothes

doing, showing, and telling;
the path
of least restriction
has always been well traveled

this is what I was feeling when
I stumbled once again upon the thought
that good children
sometimes come from bad parents

the unhelped child
can become independent
the harassed child
can become resourceful

so it was that
in the Winter of '07
I prayed against
the cold and the irrevocable change

my God
give me warmth; and please
form what's left of my splintered hope
into the next, renewing season

a number of primes

almost every year
I encounter yet another
peak in experience
or ability

one of my most
memorable romances
took place
in fifth grade

I remember
brilliant sunshine blurring
the view through the windows
at the front of the drugstore . . .

. . . as I eagerly carried
the box of chocolate pieces
—they were Nielsen's—
up to the till

but a dozen years sentient
I was overwhelmed
by new feelings of
unprecedented intensity

I probably peaked
as a runner a year or two
after I had stopped
playing sports

in my early twenties
I won a foot race
against my athletic
younger brother

our impromptu
two man race was run
from light pole to light pole
in the cool, wet dark

amazingly,
my fast-twitch fibres
must have continued to develop
without me

looking back,
I may have been most useful
when I taught Sunday School
in my thirties

for fifteen or so years
no one else offered to teach
the ever-changing junior high class
and so I continued on

I refined my teaching
method over the years,
and, in the end,
simply read the Bible out loud

nowadays when I meet
former students I am content
knowing that I strove to respect them
as adults before they were

I had always been impressed
with how
quickly my economics adviser
edited my thesis

in one afternoon the research
contained in a passel of creased,
mix-matched pages went from
almost unrelated to focused

twenty-five years later,
I actually wowed myself
editing a child's university paper
with similar skill

I had lost almost all my speed
on the ice rink, but
apparently as a reader and writer
I had kept getting better

at some point, maybe soon,
my slowing synapses
will fail to keep up with what I chance
to learn each day

if I am witness to that change,
I pray that I will revel
in my new, hopefully more caring,
perhaps grandchildren, prime

little bang

where I live
we are sufficiently comfortable
to take time
to try and understand (full stop)

all of us
enjoy our small-
to-great pleasures
of body and soul

some of us accept
that ultimate meaning, and
the resolution of the great mysteries
rests with God

I've often said
that the problem
of the birth
of the universe

is only a problem
for someone
who does not accept
there is a God

people who don't acknowledge God
have the problem
of trying to explain
how it all got started

according to my observations
anti-God people
are at a loss to decide
what really is important

they appear
willing to mingle
meanings
of very different magnitudes

they treat less important meaning
and lesser mysteries
as being the equal of ultimate meaning
and the great mysteries

for this reason, solving even little mysteries
can prove to be satisfying,
at least for a while:
"I finally figured this puzzle out"

and when the resolution of mysteries
proves elusive, people who don't
embrace God often turn
to the calming images of art

or, they begin the endless study of
one's self—you may have heard it said,
as I have, that such a study can apparently
provide endless fulfillment

back to the Big Bang,
if you can't explain the Big Bang
you focus on
something you can explain

such as what happened
in ever smaller
fractions of a second
after the Big Bang

in the case of life,
if you are haunted
by an inexplicable death
you can, say,

focus on yard work,
or paint a picture
of an old man slouching away
from the village

on poetry (#4)

poetry
conjures up emotion,
place or time, or makes me
stop and think

the best poems are quotations
from a conversation
where there was
an unlimited time to reply

that's from a reader's
perspective,
the outside
looking in

the other
perspective is the poet's,
from the inside
looking out

by some measure
what I write
isn't poetry at all
it's just a collection of thoughts

looking out (from the inside)
poetry tries
to provide
an explanation

sometimes insights
arrive unannounced
before you've thought
about the problem

other times you
write to describe
a joy that
confounds

still other times
the matter at hand
is the faceless
opponent/ally, solitude

solitude forms
with the awareness
of life's
contradictions

contradictions
that can be as basic as
"I don't do what
I have a mind to do . . .

. . . because
I do not have
the heart to carry it
out against myself"

the act of writing
a poem allows me
to feel like I'm responding
in a more permanent way

and, of course,
there is always the fun of coding:
each poem a puzzle
with a hidden message,

the protective cover
made up of ellipses,
metaphors, and Byzantine
changes in theme

sometimes, though,
it seems as if poetry responds
to my solitude almost
without my involvement

as if the real author
is a jazz-worded muse
who is intent on
disregarding my suggestions

if I had a different make-up
I expect my response
to solitude would
be, well, less poetic

if I had a Roman heritage
I could draw upon my *dignitas*
and move stoically
towards what lies ahead

if I were more ambitious
I could dismiss my misgivings,
and re-focus
on the project at hand

if I was more inclined
to fashion I could
remind myself of
my reliance upon design

for me, though,
it is the thinking and
writing of poetry
that helps me to understand

Paul comments on
our powerful ability
to understand our world
in his letter to the Romans

"For since the creation
of the world God's
invisible qualities his eternal
power and divine nature—

have been clearly seen,
being understood from what
has been made, so that men
are without excuse."

perhaps someday I will
endeavor to describe how these
selfsame words
meet solitude head-on

in church today

people who are okay
weren't in church today
only broken people
bothered to show up

most obvious
were the five or so guys
who must have gotten up early
at the recovery house

you see, church starts early,
even earlier it seems when it's cold and wet
that crew must have been pretty low
to have made it on time

they know who they are
and the rest of us
know who they are
but it doesn't matter in church

one row over
and a little ways down
there was a contingent
from grandma M.'s family

S. told me that grandma M.
died early this morning,
which means the family
must have been up all night

I haven't seen grandma M.'s
sons and grandsons
in church for a long time—fit,
young men are not often in attendance

as I looked around it hit me
that today, maybe especially
today, everyone in church
was pretty much busted up

there was a good representation
of the set number of things
that can go wrong: health,
money, relationship, etc.

on my count, within four pews
there was cancer, a failed marriage,
a business setback, and several
missed mortgage payments

all of which meant
that there wasn't anything
fake or distracting
about church today

it wasn't a revue,
or a thought provoking play,
or even a baseball game:
"go Angels, go"

it's rare
to find a place
where culture
is so uncomfortable

where worship,
flawed as it must always be,
is so much more real than
any documentary could show

why was I in church today?
a watched sparrow,
I sought God's mercy
as I recovered from a fall

tunneling through

in order to answer questions about faith
I have tried to tunnel through
to the heart of the Christian message
taught to me since my birth

I continually return to John 3:16,
—undoubtedly the first verse
I was asked to memorize—which says
you are simply required to believe

friends of mine who are not steeped
in the Christian tradition
have asked me
what they need to believe in

so I turn to Peter . . .
long before St. Peter's Basilica
and two millennia of tradition
Simon Peter was in the presence of Christ

Christ asked Peter,
"Who do you say that I am?"
Peter's answer
tells us what we must believe

Peter said,
"You are the Christ,
the Son of the living God."
Christ approved of the answer

the power in this belief
is that once you accept Christ's deity
His words are seen as pure truth,
Truth

we all long for meaning
and its senior colleague, Truth
to help guide our
partly formed consciences

not surprisingly,
when we hear Truth
it makes perfect sense
(to test this, consider first . . .

. . . the power of the greatest
commandment, to love God,
and, then, the power of the second,
to love our fellow man)

while the requirement of belief
is the Biggest question
next up is the role of evil
which paces restlessly nearby

I *am a* Chevrolet

I am a Chevrolet
and so I always buy
a Chevrolet

my lineage is the lineage
of a Chevrolet:
to understand me, and the car,
you have to go back
a hundred years ago, or so,
back to when roads
were made of dirt,
oil came from Texas, and
Europeans were resented

back to when light and heat
were the same thing—the light
of a fire, the heat of a fire—back
to when people could pick up
and move to start a new life,
and not just try to start a new life

back to when chrome was the
preferred option and
not just added weight,
to when empty streets
accepted metal fins
and windows were scrunched
in pursuit of style,
to when the most common remark
was you could shoot that
engine and it would still run

today, although it is changing,
what with some of the plastics
coming from here and some of
the metal coming from there,
a Chevrolet is still
a lot like me

Chevy's are made by me,
or rather by people like me,
who live in towns like me, watch
things on t.v. like me, and have
ambitions like mine, including
even now and again
the ambition to do more than
is expected (but, like me, of course
not always)

why would I ever
buy anything other than a Chevrolet
made by me or by my brother?
to buy something made by someone
else, somewhere would be like using
someone else's arm to turn the key in
the ignition . . . it would be an indictment
of someone like me, it would be an
indictment of me

fast-moving, schooled consumers,
who have forgotten their kin,
assert without a conscience
that automobiles are inanimate chattels,
but they aren't,
they represent us,
they are us, and
I am a Chevrolet

don't be late

win or lose tomorrow, it was a stellar year
for the soccer team affectionately dubbed "la
viola cinghiale" by our Italian guide last fall

(maybe you had to be there, but I still smile
at his jest that we organize the team's
game plan around Roman army tactics)

sharing a soccer shoot-out victory
with a great team is as much fun
as snorkeling in Hawaii

great teams have players
who believe in each other and step forward
when they learn they don't have a keeper

great teams don't give up
on coaches who clearly
don't know what they're doing

players on great teams
smile during practices and at the end of games
no matter how deep they are into a losing skid

now that the year is almost over
I'll tell you what I've learned
and also let you in on my secret strategy

I've learned that speed kills,
you can't coach courage, and
good players don't get caught with the ball

I've also learned you should always pretend that
you're playing a sibling you really want to beat
but who you'd never want to hurt

and I've learned not to look back on a game
when it's over, but instead to immediately
start planning for the game coming up

and, of course, I now realize that fundamentals
win games, you should practice at game speed,
and fitness is king (or queen)

it turns out I did have a secret strategy
and, no, it wasn't following Colin's advice
to stop tinkering with the line-up

all year I've tried to coach a different game
(it's funny how these words could be a one line joke
about how little I know about the beautiful game)

the mantra, "coach a different game"
reminded me that soccer can only ever be
one small part of life

and even when
things go horribly wrong on the pitch
the sun will rise and set as usual

never forgetting, though, that like every
other part of life, you get the most out of soccer
by playing it absolutely full on

so, thanks a million for the year, and
if you trust me at all, trust me when I say,
"I treasured your friendships"

you're right, I was joking about that "win or
lose" thing; Starbucks will be on me after the win,
and the next practice will be on Tuesday

. . . don't be late!

the mighty Fraser

on
several
occasions
this summer
the first thing
I heard from the

radio alarm by
my bed

was an information
bit telling me that a
drop of oil can
contaminate a million
drops of drinking water;
the message that clean water
is so important that we'd
be fools not to avoid polluting
it with oil seems too obvious
(though, the one to a million
does drive the point home)

in my view, though,
the much bigger problem
is that in a good year
far more than a million salmon

—who not only drink water
but actually live in it—swim
up the greatest salmon-bearing
river in all the world; that river,
the mighty Fraser, is right here
in British Columbia; among this
multitude of fish are many sockeye,
the most prized salmon of all,
who continue swimming up stream
to spawn in the Adams River;
how do we greet these majestic fish

that honour us with their annual loyalty?
we gasoline and diesel-power boat to
our unrestricted delight on the Shuswap
Lake and also on the Adams Lake:
"Have fun friends!" and as a result
each second of each minute of each day,
except presumably a few days in winter,
an untold number of drops of oil mix
with the head waters of the Shuswap
Lake and the Adams Lake and then
mindlessly follow the water's flow down
into the Little River and then down the
Little Shusap Lake and then down the
Thompson River, which in about fifty miles

        feeds the mighty Fraser, that world famous
        river whose mouth is at the Pacific; I fully expect
        to awaken some day soon and hear on my radio that
        a billion drops of oil, or so, did what millennia couldn't
        do: namely, kill the very last fish who began the journey up
                  the mighty Fraser

a collector of words

I don't want to be a collector of words . . .

. . . or obsessed with austerity,
an observer of fashion always thinking about brand names,
a master storyteller,

or consumed by thoughts of traveling the world,
someone who lives for political causes,
a father exclusively promoting his children,

or inclined to revisit the same set of memories,
a golfer whose handicap is on the way down,
a fearless opponent, a tattoo artist,

or, more broadly, a person lost in the pursuit of any artistic skill,
especially if I start to believe that art—which is often
the most comfortable, consuming interest a person can have—
could very well be, the beginning and end of all things;
you can understand how such a delusion sets in:
just to write down an idea down gives it some significance,
the self-sufficiency of an art form further accreting
around its history, its terminology, and the symbolism
and other types of intelligence visible in better art,

or the world's greatest fan,
an investor with a knack for making brilliant investments,
a researcher on the verge of a breakthrough,

or consumed by a hobby, whether it's restoring a '69 Chevy or completing
a network of scale trains in my basement,
a person known for dedication to his profession,
an irreplaceable teammate,

or a developer with finalized plans for ten acres,
a baker of fruit pies with notable crusts,
a tailor offering a quick turn-around, and reasonable prices,
even a candlestick maker, assuming they still exist . . .

. . . I don't want to be a collector of words if it distracts me from
what is really important.

paying off my motorcycle

Motorcycles are seen as the modern maverick's mount, at least by those who ride them. Young men buy a motorcycle as soon as they can rustle up the cash. Older men have to wait until their children approach self-sufficiency, their careers plateau, and there is an opening on their credit line. Oh yeah, older men also need a few clear days to dream about how buying a motorcycle will re-invent their youth.

I first saw my future motorcycle in a full-page contest advertisement. I hadn't owned a motorcycle for years and I couldn't identify what make of bike I was looking at. The bike, though, seemed to be a good blend of heritage and sport. In short order, and after one of my brothers had assured me there was really only one make of motorcycle, I gave in and bought my new bike. The rest of my story dates from the day I picked it up.

I had agreed to meet a friend at a pub where he was having lunch. My friend didn't know I was going to show up riding a motorcycle. When I arrived, I parked beside an even larger bike. After I had turned off the ignition of my bike, the owner of the other bike—who wore leathers and was obviously quite seasoned—came up to me in a friendly manner and said, "You're doing it wrong. You always back your bike in." I explained to him that I'd just picked the bike up an hour earlier. We talked a bit longer, after I had re-parked my bike by backing it in.

I went inside to meet my friend. A few minutes later my motorcycle friend came over to our table, smiled, and said, "There are a couple of more things I should tell you. First, remember that from now on you don't have to pay any cover charges. Second, you should take that off your helmet." He proceeded to point to the bright orange price sticker that was still on the top of my helmet. The joke was only partly on me since I actually never go anywhere there is a cover charge.

Eventually I took my lunch companion outside to see my new bike. As we walked by the bigger bike I noticed it had a sign on it that confirmed, how shall I say this, a connection between the owner and a fairly large, motorcycle-based organization. My motorcycle friend happened to be outside as well. He said, "You know, you really should lose those cords." My old friend looked down at the corduroy pants I was wearing and started laughing. My motorcycle friend continued, "Oh yeah, and if you get some custom pipes people will hear you coming." His final comment, a story really, which I choose not to repeat in its entirety, was a description of how his life changed after he had purchased his new motorcycle; and how I could expect my life to change, especially my luck with the ladies.

I have always thought that these exchanges—which confirmed how out of touch I was (or had become)—were priceless; or, at least went a long ways towards paying off my motorcycle.

ol' snakeskin

who wouldn't want to still be racing
down the sidewalk at the speed
of a young girl
or boy determined
to be on time for a
birthday party or
a pick-up game of any sport

the problem is that
as you age you become increasingly
aware that although you'd like to think
you are still active,
there are fewer things
to pursue, which suggests
you are more ol' snakeskin than snake

when you chance to roll
the memories of glory days around,
like small stones in your hand,
you are reminded
of the developing shortage
of anticipations, few with a character
to rival those of the past

for the person getting older,
the days of today
can be mainly seen
as being made up
of recasts of events from earlier on:
all you see or do is a
reshaping of original experiences

. . . almost without fail, once early each year when
I step outside I become suddenly aware of the unique smell
that signals for me the first day of spring
I usually do not bother to try and differentiate
the confluence of contributing smells,
all heated by the new sun,
that make up the smell of a break in the seasons,
but, upon reflection,
I believe that the smells include
exposed gravel and soil, puddles,
rotting vegetation, and fresh plant growth
interestingly, each year when I first smell spring
I don't think about the spring that is just underway,
but instead I am always transported back
to the springs of my childhood
in my old hometown
many years ago . . .

this is not to say that
there is nothing new in each life,
no matter how old,
or to overlook the comforts
of faith, family, society, beauty,
tradition, etc., and so perhaps
"ol' snakeskin" is too lifeless an image

moreover, weaknesses can act
as strengths; like when the blurring
of memory allows us
to re-enjoy so many things
in a way that would otherwise
become dull: try eating, and still enjoying,
lemon pie for seven days straight

yet, each age has its own neighbours
which, it turns out, are different
from those that populate
the other stages of life, the differences
most pronounced when an
adult contrasts his or her life
to the lives of children

desiring ever greater happiness
won't make it so
likely the best you can do
is to accept that each part of life
is temporary and that in time
you run out of
bigger and better

as you age you may want to
remind yourself
now and again
that you're probably feeling
exactly how you should:
not perfectly comfortable
in your skin, your ol' snakeskin

thirty million dollars

it seems absurd to have to
argue in favour of mom and apple pie
and for having children
but we thought we needed to acquire

the power to carefully plan our children
as a result of the physical law known as "the see-saw
of advances and retreats" which applies to
all mankind's so-called progress

this law ensured that
there would be a cost to pay
for eliminating our predators,
both large and microscopic

because now there would be
too many of us
(I'm told budgies live 10 years in a cage
but only 2 years in the wild)

so I'm not shocked when
a conversation with young adults
rounds the corner on
the benefits and drawbacks of having children

of late, I have started
my remarks with the statement
that my three children are worth
thirty million dollars

I continue by saying
that the largest amount of money
I can imagine dealing with
is ten million dollars

and since each of my children
must be worth that much or more
together they must
be worth thirty million dollars

I then go on to say that
this knowledge has a calming affect
whenever I consider my monthly expenses
and the household debt

(although it is beyond indelicate
to refer to money when discussing life,
I ask for a moment more
to make my point)

your rebuttal might be
that numerous things
—including solitude—
are priceless

and therefore,
according to my standard,
are worth the upper limit
of ten million dollars

I would then respond
that while, with only the rarest
of exceptions, all parents
hold their children dear, . . .

. . . it may be necessary from time to time
to remind society, as a whole,
about the true value
of children

all living things
need to be continually renewed, and who can doubt
but that children are the fresh shoots in spring
that renew humanity

don't think of this renewal
as merely re-stocking
the ranks of the already teeming masses,
no!

think rather of this renewal
in terms of the power
children have to clear
mankind's ever-clouding vision of itself

Christ said, "You have hidden
these things from the wise
and the learned and revealed them
to little children."

He also said, "Whoever
humbles himself like this child
is the greatest
in the kingdom of heaven."

it seems that the simple faith of children
enables them to accept God's love
let me always be with children
seeing, hearing and understanding as they do

the young aren't fatally distracted by their
own importance; instead, they are engaged
by the new beauty of their world
and their bursting lives within it

contrast the fascinations of adults
as adults grow older they focus increasingly inward:
green leaves, turning brown, itemizing everything,
even the processes of their own death

as if by studying yourself even more,
digging ever deeper in your own psyche,
you will be able to uncover some hidden,
ultimate truth about yourself

(I say,
good luck, on being able
to know more
than you can know)

thinking further on it,
I am certain that answers to the ultimate questions
will never be found in weekend editorials
or even books of ideas

rather, I am convinced that many
of the important answers lie in wait near
expressions of love; like when we do
something special for a child

" . . . the boy Peter, already 'father to the man',
can only hope to grow younger still. "

at transition's edge

out here near salt water,
at transition's edge,
there is wave upon wave
of epochal change

big changes track behind
the small changes, which include
graying attendees
at youth events

"We decided to move farther out
when we realized
ours were the only kids
in the cul-de-sac."

"I find that
I have to put it in writing now,
something I never
did before."

"What's meaningful?
I guess the here and now,
and choosing
to rely on people."

who we are and what we believe
seems to have gone
from butterfly
to caterpillar

after the transition
the very last acknowledgement
of our Maker
can be expected to come . . .

. . . from an athlete
who is surprised by his own
God-given talent,
as if watching himself from a distance . . .

. . . or a mother cradling
a dying child,
or a farmer standing alone in drought-stricken fields,
too tired to cry

there were innumerable
stories of private faith
in the face of mystery
in the years preceding the transition

but different stories are told
in a man-made world
where, we think, we control it all,
from stock prices to climate change

basic meanings change too
the phrase "go to hell" now just gauges anger;
and "kingdom come" is a place
to where you are comically blown

so it is when
the fat cat of easy money
(and its companion, a little knowledge)
rubs up against us

from what I see,
economic wellbeing works quickly to subvert
the ideals of the diligent
and anyone else who shares in the happy fortune

and only a bona fide whacko
could argue against
the western world's commitment
not to leave any voter behind

the trick is, you bare a window overlooking purposelessness
when you alter the equation
that God's providence, and hard planting,
grow a garden

social welfare is needed, obviously!
and there's little wrong with expecting as, respectively,
family and citizenry,
inheritances of money and roads

the irony, though, is that each such gift
can be as deadly as a seppuku wrapped in holiday paper
which can only mean the first world
will finish last

chrome appliances, a shorter
work week, and a guaranteed early retirement
—freedom at five-five, six, or as late as seven
each a colorful lure with a barbed hook

the premise:
that comfort and predictability
lead to injury or worse clearly has no commercial value
and so stays on the shelf, unsold

but what about the
disorienting chasm
between what people think they are buying
and what they are actually getting?

            back before the transition
            there was a western world that
            is now dismissed as provincial, parochial,
            patriarchal, and superstitious

            in that world it was faith
            and family—yes, in that order;
            and in that world often young people chose
            to live other than for themselves

I recently met an anachronistic,
young missionary couple;
they were well spoken,
but had a puny net worth statement

I asked, why did you go abroad
the husband said that he had decided to go
after being challenged to articulate
what he was willing to give up for God

they were both Bible translators
and had met on the field
I asked if there is running water
for them and their children—they said no

it also turns out that there is no electricity,
except for what can be generated by solar power;
and that both malaria and AIDS
are prevalent

I asked them if they felt
they had done some good
they smiled together, and said
they thought so and were going back

sometimes late in the day,
composed and careful-planning
comfort seekers smile knowingly
and refer to "the way of all things"

which means,
don't forget you're all that matters,
but also don't lose sight of the fact
you won't be around forever

during the transition expect the construction
of life-defying casinos
to distract us from the dry rot in
empty church pews and baby rooms

a religious experience

is there a theory
that says experiencing
heightened emotions
provides a life-giving tonic?

our unnumbered emotions
are as different
as plain happy is
from plain sad

the mildest emotions
circle the day to day
of Monday to Friday,
with Saturday off

the strongest emotions
accompany the
events that are recognized
to be important

first, there is first love
blasting its emotions
of desire, happiness and
continual expectancy

and what about the emotions felt at
a marriage include joy,
anticipation and acceptance
(and possibly fear)

And those felt at the birth of a child
is attended by parental love,
but also amazement
and interest

on the death of a friend
sorrow is marked
by both sweet and
somewhat bitter memories

an event that
is referred to less often
(if at all), at least in what
I have been reading, . . .

. . . that is saturated
with emotion is
is the worship of God
on Sunday morning

on a good Sunday,
I shed a different kind of tear,
the first tear always
forming in my right eye

my tears are accompanied
by other identifiable
physical reactions, like warm
shivers from my forehead to my knees

thinking on it,
Sunday's emotion includes
feelings of a love of majesty,
acceptance, humility and wonder

as far as I know
I have only ever felt
these exact emotions
on Sunday morning

against desolation

*"For who among men knows the
thoughts of a man except the man's
spirit within him."*
I Corinthians 2:11

it is impossible
to separate the two narratives
that define us: our lives, and our thoughts about our lives,
with emotions somewhere in between

our lives,
as lived out day to day,
would, though, appear to be the primary narrative
as this is what we do and what is done to us

and it would seem
that nothing could ever be more true,
more real,
than our actions and what affects us

the reality of our lives
—which could be called the breathing narrative—
is somehow different from, but intertwines,
the other narrative: our thoughts about our lives

the other narrative is, in part,
an editing room (or a de-briefing room)
wherein we assess each act, whether in the past,
occurring now, or anticipated

the other narrative
must also be the place
where we host
the muse, promoting creativity in all its forms

is the other narrative
our heart, mind, conscience, or soul?
or is it something altogether different?
who knows the complete answer?

the ongoing mystery
of the other narrative
is how mere thoughts
can override our physical impulses

why draw any lines
to limit our animal instincts:
why not always pleasure? what about
the human traits that exceed instinct:

whence love,
altruism,
honor,
being true to one's self?

explaining away the potential power
of the other narrative is an awkward problem
for those who don't believe
there is a communicating God

when you believe there is a God
standards of conduct can be understood as
God-inspired (living expressions of faith)—
which is world's away from the instinctual

if you don't believe there is a God, everything
is arbitrary and it would seem that the only possible reason
to consider your actions are the consequences
that could track through to you or yours

consider
the difference between
loving those who love us, and
loving our enemies

I recently saw an evolutionist on t.v.
explain, in a clammy way it seemed,
that helping total strangers
is consistent with evolution

his explanation was that random acts of kindness
are mistakes ("evolutionary misfirings")
by individuals who confuse the recipient
with someone who can aid them in return

I would never argue
that goodness is the private reserve
of religion-spouting folk,
or that there is not an inclination towards friendship

but I would argue that a certain type of goodness
is evidence of an acknowledgment
there is a God, an acknowledgment
that involves the "other narrative"

if God is not our witness
then surely the breathing narrative
must most times
overwhelm the other narrative

aspiring only to better self,
Nietzsche-like we would connive on,
strive on, subject only to
the broad control of social contracts

live—but don't necessarily let live—
don't second-guess temporary satisfaction
eat, drink and all the rest,
at least until knocked back by the group

if God is not our bread of life
life starts, and has to end, with theses like those of
Sartre ("man must rely on his own fallible will and moral insight")
and Dawkins (evolving animals in a cold, atomic world)

interestingly,
these soulless views
are not generally promoted in our daily interactions,
especially with our children

and they stand in contrast
to the creativity, optimism and hope
we feel
when we are most alive

I have watched rich, godless men face death
they don't need to acquire more wealth
and yet they continue to work
until almost the day they die

when pressed, a rich, godless, dying man
is likely to assert that that he would like to
help set up a family member or leave some kind of mark
—such is self-actualization in the West

if he comments further,
he might say that although his death is imminent
this is what he does to give his life
a daily purpose, which is a form of pleasure

and who can deny that like sharks
who must keep moving forward to survive
we are built to keep doing . . .
doing something

however, I argue against desolation

in the written room

there is
a fairly large mammal
taking up space
in the written room

that needs
to be confronted, namely,
the physical attraction
between the sexes

this powerful attraction
constantly hijacks our thoughts
and manipulates
our ambitions

so, what are any of us
who strive to be semi-pure
—to be somewhat good—
to do?

it's especially tricky
because sex is obviously integral
and our thoughts upon it
corrupt so easily

if that wasn't enough
it turns out that
what we think may as well be
what we do:

"'But I tell you that
anyone who looks
at a woman
lustfully . . .

. . . has already
committed adultery
with her in his
heart.'"

Christ told His followers
they needed
to love God
and love others

it follows that somewhere within love
there must be a defense against
the wanted/unwanted elephant
. . . so what is love?

thinking on it,
love is, in part,
a decision to deny self,
to narrow our experience

my favourite
stories include those
where my contemporaries
chose against youthful temptation

the archetype
of these stories
is the story of Joseph
and the jailer's wife

you may remember,
that Joseph declines
to give in to the sexual advances
of the jailer's wife

this story, and each of the
unique yet overlapping
modern takes,
is a classic story

in a good story,
a believable and powerful
evil contests with a believable
and powerful good

an additional quality
of a classic story is
the uncertainty about the outcome
until the very end

differences

there are some
things you just know;
thoughts that seem
to be worth writing down

thoughts that
you expect to be of value,
perhaps tomorrow,
in an unexpected way

one of my thoughts
is that men are different from women
not to gratuitously frustrate them
but for historical reasons

men needed
to be bull-headed to
protect the cave
or cottage

if they hadn't been bull-headed
they'd have turned and run
at the first sight
of a saber-toothed lion

also, men needed
to be inconstant, flighty even,
to ensure that new lands
would be discovered

C. Columbus obviously felt
that heading out on a dark sea
was his only chance
to make something of himself

another one of my thoughts
is that there are
irreconcilable differences
between all of us

"I like this more than that"
says the first; the second "likes that"
and the third likes
something else entirely

these differences
mean that people, given enough time,
mostly get bugged beyond measure
by other people,

which makes marriage
—a long term coming together
of two of the most unlike types—
an impossible living arrangement

. . . it is funny, though,
how the durability
of the institution so easily puts a lie
to an otherwise useful thought

bad from good

and yet again
I've learned
what I didn't
think I would

that there is
so much bad
that can come
from something good

imagine
helping someone out,
an act
of altruism,

without
a string attached,
not even
one condition

"good"
that is as good
as ever
a good began

no bad
can come of that!
. . . you would
do well to think again

one thing that
might go wrong
(results can be
contrary)

is that what
you've done
won't fix the
beneficiary

another thing
that can occur
is that someone else,
somewhere

will agree
the gift was helpful
but won't think
that it was fair

"And what
about my gift?"
can sometimes
be their thought

this might
be asked out loud
but usually
it is not

now to finish with
a maxim,
a warning
that is well met,

what comes
from doing good
may not be
what you expect

tunneling through, continued

of course God knew
the consequences
would be beyond
what we could ever understand,

but He still allowed us
to have so much,
God's First Gift,
to be in His image

I used to think that thoughts and
language were mankind's most
important abilities, but now I realize
how limiting this assessment is

you have to think
as broadly as you can
to comprehend
the glory of being human

what people can do
what people are
the Great books,
the Great emotions

the great buildings,
the great adventures
the great athletes
the great ideas

the ability to stand up straight,
but it is more than that
it is the ability to split the atom,
but it is much more than that

the ability to care
about orphans
halfway
around the world, and

the ability to begin
to understand an artist's rendering,
but it is still
much more than that

now the trick: coupled to
these almost unimaginable abilities
is the greatest possible
sense of independence and self-worth

Can we fly?
"I'm booked to go to Maui next week."
Can we bring someone back to life?
"Quick, hand me the defibrillator!"

with so much power
we are almost unable
to remember that
we are the created and not the creators

the Greek gods in literature
were given human qualities
because they were us,
and not because we were them

so like those fickle gods
we make decisions
that are not staked out
by any known morality;

some of our uncaring edicts
are insignificant
others, however, are so large
they forever scar our history

the heartless power
of the self-appointed
has an old tradition
on this spinning sphere

going back as it does
to the fallen angel
who knew that knowledge
would allow us to "be like God"

"You said in your heart
I will ascend to heaven;
I will raise my throne
above the stars of God."

when our race
accepted the serpent's recommendation
to take fruit
from the tree of knowledge

the path of humanity
was forever altered
as we were sent out
of perfect Eden

the change was so great
(and seemingly unalterable)
because with this knowledge
we had so inhabited our image,

likened as it is
to God's image,
that we could no longer see
beyond ourselves to God

think well on this
how mere money can distract us
"it is easier for a camel
to go through . . ."

imagine
just how distracting
are our majestic forms
and abilities

God knew that our self-admiration
would have to be confronted
(we would have to suffer)
if we were to remember Him,

and yet He still chose
to create us in this glorious way
and forewent the alternative to make us
something less than what we are

He could have made us animals
who are less able to think and to do
yet He was not swayed
from making us in His image

God knew how this would affect us,
and that it would take
an intervention
of supernatural proportions

to overcome the distorting affect
of our God-like power
and enable us to look past ourselves
and see His glory

the correction could only come
from pain and suffering,
which was, of course,
God's Second Gift,

       the first metaphor is that God crafted
       a corrective lens to fix our myopia from a molten,
       glassy mixture of chaos, tragedy and pain
       without reference to the physics of this world

a lens that could only be effective
if the amalgam included endless war,
the banality of private evil, an onslaught of diseases,
and everything that causes pain and cannot be explained

the second metaphor is God is our combatant
all-knowing and of unequal strength
who knocks down those in His image
not once, but continually, to force us to submit to Him

knocked down with the realization that some things
are so horrible that they cannot be explained away
knocked down with the knowledge
that we control so very little

to repeat, the great irony is that
this act of love is inextricably connected to death
(including the death of His son)
and destruction

note that God did not love
all of His creation this well
—contrast God's dealings
with Satan

you see Satan,
who seems to have, like us,
a similar likeness to God,
was not shown the same corrective love

instead, Satan lives the worst
of all lives, untrammeled by earthly setbacks,
he cannot make the long journey
back to the temple of the Lord

you might think it sounds as simple
as God getting our attention
by making us fearful or mad
—"Why me!" (or you, or them),

God knowing
that only when our appetites are unfixed
will we take up more noble thoughts
and remember to pray

however, were we able to stretch
our minds enough
we would realize
just how misguided it would be

to suggest that the God
of the Bible is not affected
by the groaning
of His very creation

The question has always been,
"Why is there pain and suffering?"
There is, it turns out, a far
bigger question:

Are we capable of comprehending
even part of God's great love,
a love which can be seen
in both of the gifts He gave us:

God's First Gift, to be in His image,
and God's Second Gift,
to be drawn back to Him
with pestilence, war, famine and death?

false spring

what if
you had to sieve the body
from the soul
to rid worry?

soul (spirit) . . . body . . .
to an onlooker
our human forms must look like
cells under a microscope

each cell the same,
with some variation
in the shape of
each cell's walls

closer up, perhaps our fears
become visible,
and, if so, they would show
as common to us all

worry is a tyrant
whose rule
we only dare ridicule
from a safe distance

not to say that worry
does not, now and again,
relent; the problem
is it always returns

December's warm winds
are a false spring
which do not mark
the arrival of summer

worry, though, cannot
assail the othernatural
as they play games
with different pieces

Edwards Brothers, Inc.
Thorofare, NJ USA
June 21, 2011